FOCUS
ON TRAVEL

TEXT BY:
ANNE MILLMAN AND ALLEN ROKACH

PHOTOGRAPHS BY:
ALLEN ROKACH

Focus on Travel

Photographing
Memorable Pictures
of Journeys to
New Places

Abbeville Press, Publishers

NEW YORK   LONDON   PARIS

To our parents,
Sarna and David Weichman,
and Julia Rokach,

for opening our eyes to the wonders of the world

EDITOR: Susan Costello
DESIGNER: Nai Y. Chang
PRODUCTION EDITOR: Sarah Key
COMPUTER ASSISTANT: Karel Kaliner Birnbaum
PRODUCTION MANAGER: Simone René

Front Jacket. A profusion of tulips juxtaposed against houses of a nearby village conveys the essence of a Dutch landscape in spring. In this composition horizontal bands of flowers are a contrast to a diagonal trench, and the colors in the fields also may be seen on the roofs.

Back Jacket. Part of the fascination of foreign travel is meeting people from diverse cultures. To photograph strangers may require some daring as well as a knowledge of photographic technique, such as using a moderate telephoto lens to produce a revealing portrait without having to get very close to the subject. This Highlander tribesman from Papua, New Guinea, is shown wearing his colors after a ceremonial "sing-sing."

Page 1. To develop a personal style a photographer must look at people and places in terms of colors, shapes, and composition. This study in pink and white sets a young girl in her communion dress against a typical painted house in Burano, Italy.

Pages 2–3. Washington, D.C., offers more than government buildings and monuments. Here a resident enjoys the solitude of rollerskating among the trees of a manicured plaza.

Library of Congress Cataloging-in-Publication Data

Millman, Anne.
  Focus on travel : creating memorable
photographs of journeys to new places / text by Anne Millman
and Allen Rokach ; photographs by Allen Rokach.
        p.   cm.
  Includes index.
  ISBN 1-55859-371-3
  1. Travel photography. I. Rokach, Allen.
  II. Title.
  TR790.M56 1993   92-27282
  778.9'991—dc20   CIP

ACKNOWLEDGMENTS

We owe a great deal to many people whose support and assistance made it possible to create this book. We thank them all for their generous contribution of resources and time.

First among the individuals owed a debt of gratitude are a number of executives at the Olympus Corporation, who jointly provided tremendous help and encouragement. Pasquale Ferazzoli, Director of Marketing Services, gave us years of support by making the most advanced photographic equipment available on loan, so that all the photographs contained in this book could be taken with Olympus equipment. In addition, Dave Willard, Vice President of Marketing Communications, who arranged funding for a trip to photograph in Japan.

We also received invaluable help in the form of in-kind contribution of travel excursions through various organizations. The Netherlands Board of Tourism offered two trips to Holland, and we thank Barbara Veldkamp and Eline van Bon for making all the arrangements. Airfare for the two trips was contributed by KLM, thanks to Odette Fodor's assistance. Cunard, through the office of Vice President of Public Relations Priscilla Hoye, generously sponsored a cruise along the Black Sea. And Joann Osoff arranged opportunities to lecture aboard cruises to Asia and Alaska. We also appreciate the assistance of Matsuko Suematsu of the Japan National Tourist Office in planning our travels.

A special thank you to Myrna Cooper, who graciously lent us a laptop computer to use during our travels, and who has taken continuing interest in our work.

We are especially grateful to dear friends, colleagues and students who volunteered their services, both during our travels and in the editing of photographs. Thanks to David Ferguson, Ross Horowitz, Frank Kecko, Kishu Mansukhani, David Shander, Sydney Stern, and Kay Wheeler.

Of course, we greatly value the professionalism of Abbeville's editor, Susan Costello, designer Nai Chang, and production manager Simone René. They kept us on track and on schedule, despite our resistance. And they deserve credit for caring so much about producing beautiful books.

Finally, we thank Noah and Ilana Millman, who tolerated our photographic high jinks during trips we took together; who put up with our absence when we had to leave them behind; and who had the good sense to be away at college during the final stages of writing the manuscript.

Contents

6 Real People 136

7 Architecture 172

8 In Action 190

9 A Change of Pace 208

10 Great Travel Photographs 216

INTRODUCTION

Wanderlust—the love of travel—enters people's blood in unexpected and contradictory ways. In my case, I had a feverish desire to experience new places by the time I arrived in the United States at age seven.

My precocious interest began under the most inauspicious circumstances: during my parents' midnight escape from postwar Poland. In fact, my earliest memory is of bouncing on my father's shoulders as a two year old, or perhaps younger, my arms gripping his neck as we waded cautiously through a dark river near the border of Czechoslovakia. The sense of uncertainty, if not of danger, worried others in our clandestine group, but I remember it thrilled me. This adventure must have prepared me for more escapades.

Several years of meandering around war-torn Europe followed our escape as my parents tried to find surviving relatives and chart a new life. While my parents struggled, I found each relocation new and fascinating—especially meeting people of many backgrounds and languages. I was layered with languages: social survival demanded that I learn Russian from a playmate; Yiddish from my parents' literary and theatrical friends; Hebrew from my nursery school teachers; and German from neighbors and tradespeople.

There were also new foods to be savored, tastes I can conjure to this day: the sweet milk powder that we refugee children would dip our fingers into and lick off; the thick texture and unexpected tartness of sour cream and buttermilk, especially delicious with boiled potatoes; the bitter foam of beer, sipped from a stein, that left a telltale mustache on my upper lip; and the lusciousness of freshly picked cherries, a few kept for dangling over my ears like jewelry.

In Vienna my visual sense awakened, for from my perspective as a three year old, the city's grand, ornate buildings were a fairyland, especially in contrast to our dusty refugee camp. Excitement was everywhere: on the broad boulevards; in the park, with its amusements and gigantic Ferris wheel (for years I dreamed of returning to Vienna, when the wheel was repaired, to take the ride I missed); and at the magical opera, with its swirling costumes, dramatic lighting, and larger-than-life characters. A more sedate and somber impression was left by the old, bearded gentlemen and young, desperate families in dimly lit, plainly decorated rooms of our shabby residence hotel.

Three years in Germany followed, giving me a taste for the countryside and outdoor life—all intertwined with fables and folklore. How well I recall the long train rides past dense forests, which were filled, I was sure, with fiendish wolves; and the sunny climbs up the Bavarian Alps, my parents beside me like watchful bookends; and crystalline

Konigsee, echoing legends of the ghostly royal family that once occupied the nearby castle; and abandoned salt mines of the region, now tourist attractions, with their long boards sliding into the depths of the earth. Add to these experiences the pleasures of picnicking with friends in a mountain valley; watching my father quietly sketch each pastoral scene with translucent watercolors or render the features of an unsuspecting person in a telling pen-and-ink caricature; and observing my mother bargain shrewdly in the local market.

It is hard to believe that these happy scenes followed so closely after the cruel deaths of my family members and millions like them.

What made my love of travel possible, I now realize, is that my parents wanted me to live in the bright light of hope, not in the shadow of conflagration and destruction. They showed me how to take pleasure in small victories and intimate discoveries during our many travels together: finding inexpensive lodgings in New England's quaint Victorian rooming houses; luxuriating in the summer chill of a New Hampshire brook; learning how to eat lobster from a native down-Easter; moving from place to place without reservations or fixed plans, only with a sharp eye for what was interesting and an open mind toward whatever came their way.

Little did they know that from their grim and tragic past, and from their unrelenting need to economize, I inherited a great gift that continues to enrich my life.

Allen's love of travel had quite different origins. His family stayed rooted to its Brooklyn neighborhood. Except for one memorable trip to Canada with a family friend at the age of ten and summer excursions to New York's Catskill Mountains, an area the family called "the country," Allen did no traveling until his college days. In fact, he never imagined he would travel.

He recalls looking at a small globe, reading and rereading old *National Geographic* magazines, and poring over atlases, struggling to learn the names of exotic lands he believed he would never see: New Guinea, Cairo, Luxor, Bali, Bombay, Malta, the Maldives, and Antarctica. How ironic and miraculous that he has in fact visited all these places along with many others.

By the time Allen and I met, our interest in travel was well established, and we recognized it as an important link between us. We began spending weekends exploring locations around New York and New

England. Allen had recently left an academic post in geology in the hopes of launching a new career as a photographer, and these trips were meant to combine business with pleasure, adding to Allen's stock of images. As a bonus, we each were awakened to new dimensions of travel, as we photographed together.

For my part, I appreciated how Allen's keen eye was drawn to subjects I would not have noticed. His awareness was more purely formal and aesthetic than mine, and he saw pictorial possibilities where I saw nothing noteworthy. He also brought to his work a profound understanding of natural light and knew exactly how to make the most of its effects. When the pictures were developed, I was always astounded that he had created such wonderful images from such ordinary material. It was a kind of alchemy, I thought, turning dross into gold.

For Allen's part, he realized that there was much more going on than he was used to capturing on film. His approach was slow, methodical, and highly visual; mine was quick, journalistic, and highly editorial. While Allen was always on the lookout for beauty, I was drawn to the dynamics of a scene, especially to human interactions. My ability to notice events that were about to happen, anticipate where the action would be, and know when telling gestures or expressions were likely to occur proved very helpful to him. And my knack for quickly scanning new places and identifying their typical features, as well as those that were unique, made our photography more informative and efficient.

Together, Allen and I forged an unusual kind of partnership, supporting each other's continuing fascination with this vast world, traveling together, working together as a writer-photographer team, and offering workshops in travel photography in many parts of the world.

For this book, that partnership has worked very much as it has with other projects. Allen's expertise as a photographer was like a mother lode waiting to be tapped. For me to explain the complex process of photographic decision-making, I must reveal Allen's thoughts by interviewing him incessantly—both in the field when we are photographing and when we review the results. I want to know what Allen is trying to achieve with each image and how he plans to capture each one. Only then can I begin to put those ideas into words.

To help discover the diversity of images Allen needs to shoot, I often double as a scout or as an extra pair of eyes. I also research locations and assist in the often time-consuming process of juggling photographic gear. Then we collaborate on editing the text and the photographs—Allen says I'm heartless, and I say he is too sentimental.

To create this book, however, we imposed some severe restrictions on ourselves. We were both determined to experience, as much as possible, the conditions that travelers really encounter, so that our advice could be tested and the examples we gave would be authentic. Therefore, the pictures were largely shot in the typical hurried pace of a traveling vacation.

We did not allow ourselves the luxury of lengthy stays at any one place, as we would on a special assignment. Allen took many of the shots during brief camping trips, during short stopovers at ports of call on cruises, and during other hasty visits abroad. The only exceptions are the photographs taken during workshops with students to demonstrate travel and nature photography techniques.

And, while we traveled, just to keep things fair, I also devoted time to the project. I managed to draft a substantial part of the text on a laptop computer during our journeys, either in the car over long stretches of highway or whenever we had a spare hour or two after lunch or dinner.

What we hope emerges here is not just our long-standing love affair with travel, but also our conviction that there is a sensory and spiritual connection between the travel experience and the use of the camera. The very idea of travel as a leisurely activity owes much to the camera, and the early images it created of exotic people and places. And to this very day, it is the rare person who prepares for a journey without thinking of bringing back photographs.

With the newest "smart" cameras and the latest films, travel photography is becoming easier, more accessible, and more satisfying for most people. After all, many travelers were discouraged in the past by the technicalities of exposure and shutter speed, which might conflict with their enjoyment of a vacation. Today's gear is the closest thing to foolproof we have seen, and our book includes numerous photographs that illustrate that point.

But sophisticated equipment is no guarantee of memorable pictures. That is why developing a personal aesthetic and knowing how to interpret the travel experience effectively is as important—even more important—than ever before. That is a focus of this book. Most importantly we believe that travel experiences themselves are enhanced and enriched by approaching them from a photographic perspective. The very process of wanting to create expressive, telling images of travels sensitizes and emboldens people, and encourages them to approach a scene or a subject in a new way.

We hope this book inspires your travels and your photography, and that you return with terrific pictures that you will enjoy and share for generations to come.

Anne Millman
New York

1
Capturing
the Spirit of
the Trip

*"the flavor of first-hand experience . . .
is unmistakable and intoxicating."*

EVELYN WAUGH, 1934

BEYOND SIGHTSEEING

Travel and photography have been natural companions since the invention of the camera. The pioneers of travel photography lugged heavy equipment to remote, unexplored, and sometimes exotic places, recording the first "real" pictures of the sights—both natural and man-made. People were influenced by the immediacy of those images to preserve wilderness areas, to support historic restorations, and to travel to far-off lands.

At the same time, those early pictures and the many that followed have provided us with strong visual expectations: when we actually see the wonders we have dreamed of visiting, we often arrive with a measuring stick. And instead of looking at our discovery with a fresh eye, we find ourselves comparing it with what we anticipated.

Travelers with cameras have a dilemma. On the one hand, we want to record a famous sight, to document a personal appreciation of it, to show we were there. On the other hand, we would like to capture the spirit of the travel experience in an original, memorable way.

This chapter addresses the travel photographer's dilemma by showing how to take pictures with a sense of adventure and newness, wherever we may venture. By stretching and refining our powers of seeing during our travels, we can journey beyond sightseeing—toward genuine exploration.

PAGES 10-11. *The excitement of a hot air balloon flight is often best caught at the instant of takeoff, as in this shot at a balloon festival in Colorado.*
OPPOSITE. *A guidebook cannot adequately portray the loveliness of the lavender fields of the French countryside in Provence. Take time to search out such intimate and harmonious scenes by car and, especially, on foot.*
RIGHT. *A telephoto lens magnifies and extends the camera's "normal" vision. Here a 180mm lens frames the intricately eroded slopes of Bryce Canyon in Utah at sunrise.*

Portraying the Experience

One of the surest ways to give a personal dimension to your travel photographs is to show what you experienced. It is not necessary to do an extraordinary thing like climbing the Matterhorn to get spectacular photographs. In fact, ordinary events often best convey the true spirit of a trip.

Consider using the everyday act of eating, for example, as a photographic subject. Everyone eats while traveling; yet how many of us think of mealtime as a wonderful occasion for picture-taking? An eatery may be a charming café, a picnic table overlooking a canyon, or a roadside diner. Whatever makes it

ABOVE. *The instant before "takeoff" is the best time to catch the excitement of a first ride in a dune buggy, here at Coral Pink Sand Dunes State Park in Utah. A 24mm wide-angle lens elongates the vehicle to simulate a sense of movement.*

RIGHT. *Be ready for some candids in stores and markets, where people love trying things on. At this flea market in Sydney, Australia, a straw hat concession drew quite a crowd.*

OPPOSITE. *When our bus broke down in the Sinai Desert, everyone got out to push except the photographer, who decided this was a picture that had to be recorded.*

distinctive also makes it photogenic and worth photographing.

Relaxing and having fun is the purpose of vacations and travel. But it takes a little ingenuity, a lot of awareness, and some determination to be in on the fun and still take pictures of it. Do not feel that every moment has to be recorded. But if you and your companions are planning an activity, think through some moments you might want to preserve. Anticipate and prepare for the circumstances and try to include yourself in the pictures, if possible.

Even a trip's misfortunes can become great photo opportunities. You may not enjoy being drenched in the rain while hiking or having your car break down on a desert road, but a photograph of the episode will bring back fond memories years later.

Whenever possible, capture the action as it is happening. If you are in a market, snap the photo just when that comical hat is being tried on or when a blanket is being unfolded. You can ask your subject to pose or "freeze" at the crucial moment as long as the essence of the movement is spontaneous.

Games, sports, trolley rides, carousels, riverboat rides, or simple afternoon strolls all offer glimpses of the spirit of a trip. See chapter 6, "Real People," and chapter 8, "In Action," for specific photographic techniques to help capture these revealing moments.

One way to show the spirit of a trip is to combine an activity along with its location. Here three paddleboats float into the craggy Gorge du Verdon in southern France.

RIGHT. *Avoid clichés by discovering new perspectives of famous sights. The world-renowned statue of David is shown in the context of other Florentine landmarks.*

OPPOSITE. *Wandering on your own allows you to view fascinating, little-known scenes, such as this comical boar in a colorful square in Aix-en-Provence, France.*

Recording the "Sights"

The essence of travel photography is the ability to show what we see. There is no direct and inevitable connection, however, between what we see and the effectiveness of our images. The relationship between seeing and photographing is more complex and interesting.

On the most obvious level, the photographer must be "there" to see and take the picture. Yet, photographers may often overlook a potentially photogenic subject. Moreover, photographers may recognize a visual gem but lack the technical know-how to produce an image worthy of it.

To bring back remarkable photographs requires the following commitments:

1. Aim to expand the scope of your travels. This does not necessarily mean gallivanting to new places or rushing from sight to sight. Essentially it means exploring each place you visit more intensely.

   Do not limit yourself to the cues in your guidebook. Fold up your maps and open your eyes. Wander down narrow country lanes and urban alleys. Drive along "blue" highways, and walk off the beaten path. After all, the best reason to endure the expense and inconvenience of travel is to discover something new.

   The places do not have to be new to everyone, just to you. When people first view a famous sight, their reactions may run from wonder to disappointment, depending on their expectations. Coming upon a little explored sight—an unexpected discovery—on the other hand, can inspire real amazement. Your own feelings are the best barometer for having found something worth documenting.

2. Try to become visually alert to photographic alternatives. Do not be satisfied with your first view of a subject or with reproducing images you have seen in travel ads. Because clichés are the worst enemies of successful picture-taking, always try to show familiar sights from a fresh perspective.

Learn to look at each subject from different angles—from above, below, or behind; from a distance or close up; or in an uncommon light. You may personalize each photograph by creating an image that stretches your imagination.

3. Develop your technical skills. To translate a mental picture into one on film requires a mastery of your equipment. It is best to practice with it well before you take your journey. The most avoidable mistake photographers make is taking new, unused equipment on a trip. Always shoot at least one roll of film before you leave home—even if your equipment is not new—giving yourself enough time to review the results and to make any needed repairs or adjustments to your gear.

   Better yet, practice taking the kind of photographs you expect to take during your travels. That way you will know where to stand and which settings and lenses to use. Specific recommendations to help you hone your skills will be provided in Chapter 2.

Overviews

Successful photographers take many views of a scene. This leads some people to believe that the photographer is just playing the odds, taking a lot of pictures to guarantee at least one good one. In fact, these photographers are motivated by a different premise: they understand that every subject has multiple facets, and they keep taking pictures, because they keep seeing new possibilities.

If something catches your eye, take the time to consider its potential. Then, take at least a few shots to represent what you think are the most promising options. One way to develop such mental habits is to imagine the subject from three distinctive perspectives: the overview, the vignette, and the detail.

The overview is the broadest, most complete perspective. It sets a subject in its context. This is how we first glimpsed—and photographed—the Indian city of Jodhpur in Rajasthan. As we climbed towered the Meherangarh Fort, we looked down and saw that the entire city, sprawling below, was a sea of powder blue, the favorite color for the adobe houses of Brahmins in this area. Only an overview shot could effectively convey the marvel of this Blue City.

Technically, the overview is not too demanding. While a normal lens can usually encompass the entire scene, a moderate wide-angle lens can certainly include it. Focusing is simple since the subject is at infinity, but achieving the proper exposure is difficult. Because the overview often contains large bright areas of sky or such reflective surfaces as greenery, water, or buildings, exposure can be tricky. In general, meter the scene and then bracket by taking several shots at slightly different exposure settings. For slides, favor underexposure from the meter reading; for prints, lean toward overexposure.

OPPOSITE. *An overview shot from a hillside fortress overlooking Jodhpur, India, points up the powder blue color used by Brahmins to paint their stucco homes.*

A nearby rooftop provided the vantage point for this overhead perspective of a market street in Ghana.

Vignettes

In contrast to the overview, the vignette provides a closer and more intimate focus, serving to isolate visually revealing segments of a scene. Vignettes frame a portion of the whole, separating it from the surroundings as if it were suspended in space and time. Their value derives from the photographer's ability to establish a personal relationship to the scene and to project the quality of that appreciation through a carefully composed image. The photographer's imagination transforms the part into something greater than the whole. Vignettes are often unique, and, at the same time, universally compelling.

Even mundane subjects can be rich in visual possibilities for vignettes. The early twentieth-century French photographer Eugène Atget became well known for documenting ordinary life in Paris. He trained his keen eye on a host of shop windows, merchants, street peddlers, humble buildings, and simple flower pots. Czech photographer Josef Sudek shared a similar passion in Prague. Through their vision, Atget and Sudek transformed undistinguished subjects into images of high art.

That is what we all aspire to by photographing vignettes during our travels. We can discover vignettes in the city and the country; in marketplaces and on streets; in nature and architecture; and wherever people go. Technically they are not difficult to create, but they take time to search out or to identify. Most of all, they require care and thought, for they are truly products of the mind's eye.

For those new to this kind of photography, we recommend a "shoot-and-shift" process. Compose the subject from the point where you first noticed it. Then move toward it until you find another pleasing way to frame it; continue to move around, looking for other ways to compose the image. Keep shifting in search of better, more revealing views, in whatever time you have.

OPPOSITE. *The imaginative photographer is not deterred by building renovations. Here scaffolding frames a classic Florentine sculpture and adds a comic counterpoint as the hoisted female appears to be reaching up in an effort to climb higher.*

LEFT. *This abstract composition includes typical elements found in an Indonesian town—pastel-colored walls, a window with a grate, and a bicycle rickshaw.*

BELOW. *Another vignette portrays neat piles of fruits and vegetables in a West African market set against an earth-toned wall.*

An early morning light illuminates the classic lines of a dewy spiderweb.

Details

A photographic detail makes an even stronger and more personal statement than the vignette. In part, this is because it is impossible to shoot a detail without looking closely at a subject. That closeness distorts reality in a very exciting way, often changing the subject into something unrecognizable or abstract. (The art of the detail is, of course, not limited to travel photography.)

It is not necessary to shoot details just for the sake of documenting a trip. Yet the powerful interaction between the traveler and the subject that is set into motion when a photographer shoots for details often becomes the high point in a travel experience. These are likely to be the images we enlarge and hang on our walls.

Good subjects for details can be found everywhere if we pay close attention to the elements that play the greatest part in their success: color, texture, form, and line. Simple arrangements within the picture frame work best. And imagination, vision, and patience are the most important skills the photographer needs.

A variation of the "shoot-and-shift" approach helps break the habit many photographers have of taking pictures from the same distance. After taking a photograph from your customary distance, move forward and shoot again. Repeat this procedure several times, each time recomposing to emphasize the new elements you are seeing. You will come back not only with better images, but, just as important, with a richer visual experience.

TOP. *Shape, color, and texture dominate this simple composition of a haystack in North Dakota. A polarizing filter dramatizes the sky.*

RIGHT. *An overhead detail taken in an indoor Madras flower market captures the warm colors of the chrysanthemums filling the circular basket.*

UNIQUELY PERSONAL EXPERIENCES

Ultimately, travel photographs are evocative when they convey an individual's vision. Getting in touch with that vision is one of the hardest but most rewarding challenges we face as photographers.

As travelers, we often seek a parallel kind of self-discovery. We travel to gain a firsthand glimpse of unfamiliar places and ways of life, perhaps hoping to learn more about ourselves. And yet the pressure to see many places in a short time limits our ability to experience our new surroundings in truly meaningful ways.

Through photography we can take advantage of a discipline that puts an emphasis on careful, insightful seeing. When we experience our travels as photographers, we slow down and stalk worthy images. Our antennae become alert to pictorial possibilities. We are sensitive to our surroundings and learn to look for visual treasures.

This new awareness means that we are constantly interacting with what we see. We tune in to our feelings and reactions; we begin to notice elements that typify a location as well as those that are out of the ordinary. And we are open to surprises.

In truth, we look with different eyes when we travel as photographers, and the camera becomes a tool not only for preserving experiences but for enriching them.

LEFT. *A personal viewpoint may inspire some photographs: this charming entry to a pension in Mykonos helps convey the experience of an unfamiliar location.*

OPPOSITE. *To alert travelers ordinary scenes can yield memorable photographs. Here an Indian bullock standing against a wall of peeling advertisements contributes to a colorful, humorous abstraction.*

Expressing Feelings

As travel photographers, we try to recognize and respond to our feelings—as fleeting as they may be—for they signal our involvement with a situation. The task of translating our reactions and moods into visual terms is at the heart of giving our photographs a personal vision.

Several suggestions will be helpful:
1. Unless you are adept at identifying your reactions, you may have to take a moment to think about what you are feeling.
2. It is often useful to attach a label to your feelings: surprise, fear, delight, happiness, shock, relaxation, or excitement. Try to be as specific as possible.
3. Analyze the visual elements that you associate with those feelings. For example, the pattern of reflections in a pond may contribute to a sense of relaxation. The neat arrangements of fruits in a market may delight you. Or the sight of an impending storm may stir fear. If you find it difficult to pinpoint your feelings, try completing the sentence, "I feel . . . because I see . . ."
4. Focus your photographic efforts on the components of a scene that stimulated your reaction, and make them the essence of your photograph, including more only if it is necessary.

Just as our feelings and reactions are highly individual, so are the images that they can help produce.

TOP. *We found this decaying farmhouse in France intriguing. A composition based on color and shape helps create an appealing photograph, despite the broken roof.*

LEFT. *Pyramids of fruit sold in the markets of Madras were wondrous. This is just one of many fascinating sights to be discovered in marketplaces around the world.*

The tranquil mood we felt, as the sun set at Cadillac Mountain in Maine's Acadia National Park, was captured by reducing the scene to light and shadow.

California's Big Sur coastline in the rosy light of dawn is awe inspiring for those visitors willing to rise before daybreak.

Importance of the Ordinary

So much travel focuses on the wonders that attract visitors to far-off destinations that we often neglect a location's typical side, especially in our photographs. Yet it is often an image of the ordinary that most vividly recalls a place.

Pay attention to the typical architecture of a region rather than one-of-a-kind structures: photograph the brownstones of New York, not just the Empire State Building; houses along the canals of Venice as well as the cathedral of San Marco; the thatch-roofed cottages of the Cotswolds in addition to London's Houses of Parliament.

Consider photographing everyday activities: people bicycling; eating in a café, riding the local means of transportation, shopping for food and other necessities, worshipping according to local custom, and celebrating feast days and festivals of the region.

Look for typical people doing common things: vendors selling their wares; craftspeople at work; people relaxing or engaged in chores. All these make wonderful photographic subjects that reveal the details and texture of life in the place you are visiting.

A little research in advance will prepare you ahead of time, but you will still have to do some legwork to find the right subjects if you hope to get the images. It takes determination to venture away from hotels and tourist haunts into areas where ordinary people live. But those who can overcome reluctance will be rewarded with travel adventures as well as captivating photographs by which to remember them.

TOP. *These gentlemen of Sienna, Italy, are engaged in a typical European pastime—reading, chatting, and relaxing, in a café.*

ABOVE. *While peering into an ordinary West African courtyard, we found this scene of a mother bathing her baby.*

A slow shutter speed captures the early morning hustle and bustle on a typical street in Burano, Italy.

Elements of Surprise

ABOVE. *We happened upon a group of traditionally clad Japanese women at a Shinto shrine in Kyoto. Getting this shot required speedy decisions about composition, choice of lens, and exposure.*

RIGHT. *The sight of this beachfront barber in Ghana, with a sign showing his repertoire of hairstyles, was a delightful surprise.*

Even a well-planned, well-researched trip is bound to have unanticipated moments. Understanding that surprises can be photographic opportunities will make these unexpected times a delight for the adventuresome travel photographer.

By their very nature surprises catch us off guard. As a result, we rarely think about recording the moment. It may also pass so quickly that it is not possible to capture it on film. Unlike typical elements, which reoccur, serendipitous subjects require constant vigilance and some preparation to capture on film.

Here are some suggestions to increase your chances of being prepared to record surprising episodes:

1. Always carry a camera, even if it is just a small pocket camera. You never know when something picture-worthy may happen. If you choose not to take your camera along, however, do not let it bother you too much if you miss the perfect shot. Everyone needs stories about the ones that got away.

2. Take advantage of the automatic features on your camera. Since speed may be essential—especially if this is a grab shot of a moving subject—use the autoexposure and autofocus mechanisms, at least for the first shot. For nonautomatic cameras, keep the camera set for the exposure needed for the day's light conditions.

3. Do not panic. The excitement of witnessing an unexpected event often gets people so flustered that it actually takes longer than normal to set up the shot. Work calmly and methodically, doing the best you can. Remember, these are lucky shots, so do not expect perfection.

4. Take insurance photos. After the first shot, take a few more as time permits. Concentrate on perfecting the composition and exposure as you keep shooting. Many people feel so proud of getting that first shot that they forget to keep trying to take the best possible photograph under the circumstances.

We were surprised and amused when we saw this wine bottle at a roadside fruit stand in southern France where we paused for lunch.

Adjusting to Time Constraints

While professional photographers are used to working with time limitations, that does not mean they can do it easily. It does mean that they have developed some survival techniques, which can be especially helpful to sometimes rushed travel photographers who hope to bring home "world-class" photographs.

Here are suggestions for making the most of your travel time:

1. Know as much as possible in advance. Do your research at home or during transport from one location to another, and devote your travel time to experiencing the present.

2. Scout the territory. Before committing your time to any particular photographic project, learn what the territory has to offer. Take a camera along, just in case something unique crosses your path, but reserve your in-depth photographic efforts for those subjects that are worth your time. For example, walk around an area to see what it has to offer—houses, people, markets, gardens. Then go back to photograph those that are most interesting.

3. Allocate time differently for snapshots and fine photographs. Some subjects warrant a quick sketch; others demand a carefully wrought portrait. The sketch can be done speedily and with little fuss. The portrait takes more preparation, concentration, and time. If the aesthetics of the photograph are important, set aside enough time to get them just right.

4. Sometimes less is more. A great advantage of still photography is that is distills from a host of images the ones that deserve prolonged contemplation. A few outstanding photographs will bring you more pleasure and pride than a drawer full of mediocre ones.

5. Pace yourself. Know how much time you really have, then be selective. Decide which images you must have and which ones you can live without. If you pursue the ones that mean the most to you, you will not be disappointed.

OPPOSITE. *The need to arrive at the next destination should not prevent you from stopping your car if you notice something special. That was the case as we drove on a dike in Holland and lingered to photograph this surreal scene.*

ABOVE. *Alpenglow—the pink cast by the sun's earliest rays—lasts only a few minutes. It was worth getting up early to see and photograph this special sight at Grand Teton National Park in Wyoming.*

2
"Smart" Equipment

"In traveling a man must carry knowledge with him if he would bring home knowledge."

JAMES BOSWELL, 1791

ESSENTIAL GEAR

There is no end to the wonderful photographic equipment that is tailor-made for every contingency during travel. But remember: you can not lug it all with you. Dragging around too much gear takes its toll, especially if you are also trying to enjoy yourself.

Is it possible to travel relatively lightly and still be prepared to take quality photographs in most situations? Absolutely—provided you plan carefully and set priorities! This chapter will help you pack the right photographic tools.

Be sure to take only as much equipment as you can comfortably carry. Some time before your trip, pack all the gear you would like to take along. Then try carrying it for a while. If you discover it is too heavy, bulky, or awkward, you will soon resent it. Then, you will probably leave it in your hotel room, where it will do you no good—and where it may be stolen.

If you are burdened by an old, heavy camera, this may be the time to replace it with a new, lightweight model. A great improvement over their not-so-ancient precursors, today's "smart," compact cameras offer many sophisticated, built-in features that take the drudgery and worry out of photography. Many amateur photographers prefer them over single lens reflex (SLR) cameras for their simplicity and versatility. Even professionals use them regularly, especially as a spare camera, or as a handy one to tuck into a bag or pocket when more serious photography is not on the agenda. If you can, you would do well to carry a back-up camera. A small, high-tech, "point-and-shoot" model is a good choice.

If you plan to buy or borrow new gear, do so at least one month before your trip. Never travel with equipment that you do not know how to use. Test it thoroughly, shooting and developing several rolls of film. Make sure you understand all the features of the equipment and that you know how the controls work. Even old equipment should be tested, checked, and cleaned before a journey. It would be a great disappointment to face a malfunction during a once-in-a-lifetime travel experience.

Since you can not take along everything, set priorities so you have the equipment you will use most often. Anticipate the kinds of photographs you are likely to take. For a tour of

PAGES 36–37. *Today's smart, built-in meters can even handle complicated situations like this scenic in Montana's Glacier National Park. An "averaging" meter setting produced a good exposure on the sky, the water, and the land.*

LEFT. *A tripod is a must for the slow shutter speeds needed to photograph twilight scenes, such as this one in Cassis, France.*

OPPOSITE. *A purple color-correction filter (Lucalox-Type B) deepens a rosy sunset sky as a fiery-eyed bateau-mouche passes on the Seine near the Cathedral of Notre Dame in Paris.*

England's great houses, for example, prepare for indoor shots with a wide-angle lens, tripod, and flash. The opportunity to take pictures of wildlife on a safari in East Africa, on the other hand, would be lost without long, telephoto lenses and a beanbag. If space is at a premium, pack zoom lenses, which offer greater flexibility for composing than a set of fixed focal-length lenses.

Do not skimp on film. Bring enough so you will not have to replenish your supply. Far from home you may not find what you need, and you will surely pay more for it. Remember that film is probably the cheapest component of your trip. Plan on shooting two to three rolls of film a day and be sure to include types that suit the light conditions you will encounter.

Then think about your camera bag. It should be water-proof, tough enough to take some hard knocks, but inconspicuous enough not to attract a thief—an unfortunate but real consideration for all travelers. A bag with a wide, comfortable strap and roomy compartments, even if it is not specifically made for camera gear, may be more suitable than a showy case with a fancy brand name.

Cameras

Travel photography has benefitted greatly from the invention of the 35mm single lens reflex camera. Compared to the massive boxes carried by the early photographers, these tidy bundles are convenient to bring along on any excursion.

Today's 35mm SLR is still the camera of choice for most travel photography, both professional and amateur, because it is compact enough to be hand-held, and it can be outfitted with a wide variety of interchangeable lenses. All the major camera manufacturers produce high-quality SLRs with superior optics and state-of-the-art electronics capable of producing excellent photographs.

The most recent models contain an assortment of automatic features that were in their infancy only a few years ago. If you can purchase a new SLR, by all means buy one with autofocus, autowinding, and autoexposure—provided it has an override capability for special situations that can not be handled even by the "smartest" new camera. Another worthwhile feature is the built-in flash, which is automatically linked to the camera's internal metering system and saves you the trouble of carrying an extra piece of equipment.

Before you buy a camera, always check it yourself. Pick it up; notice if it feels comfortable in your hands; and decide whether the gauges, liquid crystal displays (LCDs), and controls are easy to read and to use.

Camera prices are quite flexible, so it is advantageous to comparison shop. Check the major photo magazines for mail-order listings and prices. Be an informed consumer, and you will have success resisting sales pressure to buy an overstocked item that may not suit you. And never buy a camera that you do not understand, since this is a substantial investment that should last many years.

The new "smart," compact cameras, with their built-in lens systems, do not have the full range of wide-angle and telephoto capabilities of SLRs, but they do have other advantages.

They are light, reliable, versatile, and contain many of the same high-tech, automatic features as the latest SLRs—and sometimes more.

We recommend you look for models with autoadvance, autorewind, and autoexposure, and even special modes for situations like night views, snow scenes, and portrait photography. Many feature a built-in flash with several different options: fill-in flash, normal, and red-eye reduction. We prefer cameras with a 3X zoom lens, roughly equivalent to a 28mm to 105mm zoom lens. Cameras with high shutter speeds—above 1/250 of a second—are a must if you plan to take action shots and anticipate the need to stop motion. Multibeam autofocusing frees you to concentrate on composition. One word of caution: today's autofocus cameras often can not be used for photographing clouds or reflections. Unless new models correct this limitation, rely on your SLR for such shots.

The best way to keep up with innovations in equipment is by reading the major photo magazines. The year-end issues of Popular Photography and Petersen's Photographic provide annual roundups of the newest cameras.

OPPOSITE. *Quick shots of a passing scene are simplified with automatic features for exposure and focus. Here two Venetian gondoliers on the Grand Canal are caught when they are perfectly aligned.*

RIGHT. *Point-and-shoot cameras with built-in zoom lenses make composing easy, a special boon when photographing fidgety children. These Indonesian youngsters were in an audience at an outdoor performance.*

Lenses

Using different lenses gives photographers a chance to change perspectives and to look at the world in ways that expand the capabilities of our eyes.

The various lenses available for 35mm SLR cameras are designated by their focal lengths, which determine the angle of view and the power of magnification. In general, the wider the angle, the greater the depth of field; and the greater the magnification, the narrower the depth of field.

Lenses also vary according to their speed, from the fastest at about f/1.2 up to f/8 for slower lenses. The faster the lens, the more light it gathers, making it possible to shoot under low-light conditions without a flash or a tripod. If you are shopping for a new lens, buy the fastest possible lens you can afford. Zoom lenses should be compared at full extension, since their speed may change at different focal lengths.

For travel purposes, we recommend the following lenses:

1. A standard or normal 50mm lens, sold with most SLRs. This general-purpose lens most closely approximates the perspective of the human eye. It is good for most landscapes, street scenes, groups of people, buildings, vignettes, moderate close-ups, and short-distance portraits. A popular alternative is the 50mm macro lens, which does everything a normal lens can do but has extreme close-up capability as well.

2. A wide-angle lens in the 35mm to 24mm range, with the 28mm lens preferred. Because they encompass a broader perspective, wide-angle lenses are ideal for panoramic scenes, especially where sharpness from foreground to background is important. They are invaluable wherever room for moving back is limited: indoors, in markets, on narrow streets, or between tall buildings at close range.

3. A telephoto lens. The 100mm moderate telephoto lens is the lens of choice for portraits, enabling the photographer to frame a face tightly without hovering too close to the person. The narrow depth of field of this lens can blur out an unwanted background behind the face, setting it off more graphically. It can magnify distant or inaccessible subjects, such as architectural embellishments or garden details. Longer telephoto lenses—200mm to 600mm—are needed for wildlife, for long-distance landscape shots, and unobtrusive candid photos.

4. A macro lens. Flower lovers and others with a passion for close-up photography—or an interest in developing one—will want a macro lens for its superior optics and its ability to create life-size images on the film.

5. Zoom lenses of various focal ranges. Zoom lenses are the most flexible for composing. For a single all-purpose zoom lens, we recommend one that spans 28mm to 105mm. Other zooms include the 28mm to 48mm, the 35mm to 70mm, and the 80mm to 200mm. The 35mm to 70mm is our most used lens.

OPPOSITE. *Lenses can distort reality in fascinating ways. An extreme wide-angle lens transforms a flat Dutch landscape into a long curve, exaggerating the dimensions of the swan and pond.*

ABOVE. *A telephoto lens isolates a portion of a scene at California's Death Valley National Monument, creating a strong graphic image of a dune and cloud.*

Films

Because film is so crucial to good photography, it is surprising that many people do not give it more thought. What is so important about film? In simple terms it is the film's chemical interaction with light that represents the first and most essential step in creating photographic images. Recently many new films have been introduced that are faster, sharper, and responsive to various color palettes.

These are the most important qualities to consider:

1. Film speed. Films are rated according to their speed, which is stated as an ISO number. Fast films are more light sensitive; they react with less available light, making them ideal for low-light situations.
2. Film grain. Grain refers to the size of the particles of silver oxide in the film emulsion. Fast films tend to have larger grains, resulting in photos that appear less sharp than those taken with finer grained, slow films. Some new fast films have finer grains than those of the past. Creative use of graininess can contribute to the impact of an image.
3. Color rendition. Colors reproduce differently from film to film. Some films depict warm colors such as yellows, oranges, and sepias well, while others are stronger with cool blues and greens or such pungent tones as hot pinks, reds, and purples. The exact color also depends on how

TOP. *Two versions of the Colosseum in Rome, taken at the same time, illustrate how different films affect an image. Here, film balanced for tungsten light renders the building's color as it would appear in daylight, even though it is illuminated with floodlights, and, as a bonus, it turns the night sky royal blue.*

LEFT. *This shot was taken with film balanced for daylight, turning the building yellow and the sky black.*

OPPOSITE. *For a dramatic night shot of the Arc de Triomphe in Paris, daylight film records the light of mercury vapor streetlamps as green, tungsten floodlights as yellow, and taillights of cars as red. A small aperture causes the "stars" on the streetlights.*

the film is processed. Try a few different films on a sampling of subjects and compare the results. Also, see how the same film is processed by several laboratories.

4. Film latitude. The latitude of film refers to its tolerance and responsiveness to light under high-contrast conditions—the extremes of deep shadows and bright highlights. Print film tends to have more latitude than slide film. Consequently, accurate exposure in high-contrast conditions is much more difficult when shooting slide film.

We have found that travelers select either print or slide film, mostly based on how they prefer viewing their final products. Whatever your preference, here are some suggestions:

1. Negative film for prints is now available in a wide range of film speeds. Think about the light conditions you are likely to face and use the film that represents the best match. As a general purpose film, consider Kodak's Kodacolor 200, Ektar 100, or Fuji's Reala 125. For ultrafast film, try Kodak's new Ektar 1000 or Fujicolor 400, which can be used indoors without a flash or tripod.

     But do not expect the same film to work equally well in all situations. Fast films, while sharper than in the past, are still too contrasty to handle bright conditions. Experiment with new films from Kodak, Fuji, Agfa, and Konica to check their sharpness and color. And consult the major photo magazines for color layouts providing graphic comparisons of results using various films.

2. Positive film for slides has certain advantages. It is less expensive to process than print film; colors tend to be more pungent than with print film; it is preferred by publishers for professional use; and prints can be made from the best slides for family or friends. On the negative side, it has less latitude than print film, and it is harder to make corrections for exposure in the printing process.

     Slide film also comes in various speeds, from ISO 25 to ISO 1600, with ISO 50 to ISO 100 preferred for their overall color rendition and sharpness. As with print films,

slide films respond differently in specific light conditions. For example, Fujichrome Velvia is wonderful for uniform, low-contrast light but disappointing for high-contrast light; on the other hand, Kodachrome 25, Kodachrome 64X, or Fujichrome 100 perform especially well in high-contrast conditions.

     For general photography, we recommend Fujichrome 50 and 100; Kodachrome 64 (PKR) and 200 (PKL); Ektachrome 64 (EPX) and 100 (EPZ). For the most natural and pleasing skin tones when photographing people, we recommend Kodachrome 64 and Ektachrome 64.

Films are also balanced for daylight or incandescent light. To neutralize the color of interior light, use a film balanced for the specific light source. For incandescent light or candle light, use such tungsten films as Kodachrome 40 (KPA), Ektachrome 64 (EPY), Ektachrome 160 (EPT), or Fujichrome 64 (T).

Filters

To add sparkle to your photographs, try using filters. These glass attachments come in assorted sizes to fit different lenses and generally cost from $10 to $20, although some are much more expensive because of their great precision and intricate design.

By screwing a filter onto your lens, you can add interest, variety, and a professional look to your travel photographs.

Here are the most common types:

1. Skylight filters. These filters—1A or 1B—are indispensable for protecting all your lenses from dust and grime or from accidental scratches and nicks. Their slightly pinkish color also warms the bluish tones that dominate in daylight. Many "point-and-shoot" cameras have built-in skylight filters.

2. Polarizing filters. Have you ever tried to take a picture through glass, only to get back a shot of reflections? Or have you aimed your camera at a green meadow against a bright blue sky, only to get back a dull, gray meadow against a pale, washed-out sky? If so, try using the polarizing filter, perhaps the most useful of the specialty filters made for SLRs.

A polarizer consists of a rotating glass grid that deflects, or polarizes, light that passes through it. Using a polarizing filter produces brighter, deeper-toned photographs whenever you need to eliminate reflections from nonmetallic surfaces like glass and water. It also reduces glare from shiny foliage and blue sky, and it penetrates haze. You can see the effect of the polarizer by holding it in front of your eye and turning it slowly. You will notice that some parts of the scene will darken in tone, with the greatest change visible on highly reflective surfaces or when the sun's light is at a 90-degree angle. Partial effects occur at other angles.

3. Close-up filters. These inexpensive alternatives to macro equipment come in kits of three, numbered +1, +2, and +4. They screw onto a lens to provide magnification of up to +7, if all three filters are piggybacked. That means you will be able to shoot as close as 2 to 3 inches (5-8 cm) from your subject with a normal lens.

LEFT. *A polarizing filter removes reflections from foliage, revealing the lush green of terraced rice paddies on Bali, Indonesia.*

OPPOSITE. *A polarizing filter, together with the polarizing acetate on an airplane window, creates otherworldly colors on the waters of the Missouri River, as seen from the air over Kansas City. To view the possible color effects, turn the polarizer. Avoid vibrations during aerial shots by keeping the lens close to, but not touching, the window.*

4. Soft-focus filters. If you want to achieve a romantic or mysterious effect, try one of the many soft-focus filters on the market. Always ask to see pictures taken with the model that interests you since you can not judge its efficacy by looking at the filter. Easier yet: take an old skylight filter and apply a thin film of petroleum jelly.

5. Color-correction filters. If you have ever made the mistake of shooting daylight film indoors under lights or indoor (tungsten) film outdoors, you have probably noticed that the colors, especially of skin tones, looked wrong. The reason is that each film is chemically balanced to react to a particular light. This may present a problem if travelers use the same roll of daylight film to shoot indoor and outdoor scenes.

   One solution is color-correction filters. Add an 80A bluish filter, and you can use daylight film indoors under incandescent light without risking orange faces. Add a magenta-colored FLD filter, and daylight film shot under fluorescent light is spared a greenish cast.

   Color-correction filters also do their job in daylight, subtly shifting tonalities in one direction or another. For example, the pasty white of faces photographed in bright midday light can be softened with an 81A warming filter. Or the orange skin tones caused by sunset light can be restored to normal with an 82A slightly bluish filter. For a camera without through-the-lens metering, be sure to follow the manufacturer's instructions to adjust exposure according to the filter factor.

6. Graduated filters. Most travelers face their share of less-than-perfect lighting conditions. One of our biggest worries is having to photograph a bright, nondescript sky with a shadowy landscape below. Such a scene can be rescued with a graduated neutral-density filter. These specialty filters go from light to dark gray and also come in a variety of colors. With the darker portion of the filter over the sky, the degree of contrast is reduced, and the sky takes on value through the color of the filter.

Other Accessories

In travel photography, as in many other endeavors, it is often little extras that make a big difference. With your basic equipment in the bag, let us consider this baker's dozen of other items that can contribute to your success as a traveling photographer.

1. Sunshades. These simple devices for interchangeable lenses make metering easier and more accurate, reduce flare when shooting toward the sun, and protect the lens. Each lens should have its own sunshade—the wrong shape may cause vignetting, especially with wide-angle lenses. Soft rubber, retractable sunshades are easiest to work with and offer the greatest protection.
2. Electronic flash unit. Built-in flash units are the simplest for travel. Next best is a small, powerful, automatic auxiliary unit. Not intended only for night or indoor photography, flash units are handy for fill-in flash in high contrast light, to brighten dull or low-lit outdoor scenes, and to stop motion.
3. Batteries. Today's electronic gear needs a constant diet of batteries. Start your trip with fresh batteries and be sure to bring at least one spare set for each item: camera, flash unit, meter, and winder. Keep batteries as cool and dry as possible during your travels, and remember to turn off each battery-powered unit as recommended by the manufacturer.
4. Plastic bags. Plastic bags that can be sealed keep all sorts of things clean and dry when they are not in use: film, cameras, lenses, batteries, and cleaning kit. Large plastic bags can protect your camera if you shoot in rainy or damp weather: just poke a hole for the lens, secure the bag to the lens barrel with a thick rubber band, and your weather-proofed gear is ready for service.
5. Cleaning kit. Regular maintenance is especially important

An add-on flash unit provides gentle, fill-in light for this appealing photograph of a young girl on a train in Japan. A small aperture and fast shutter speed increase sharpness while on a moving vehicle.

during travel, since we put our gear through much wear and tear. It is a good precautionary measure to spend a few minutes each day cleaning your equipment. All you need is some lens tissue, a camel's hair brush, and a rubber bulb blower. Use these to remove dust and grime. Do not use compressed air or liquid lens cleaner on lenses, because freon and other chemicals can damage the lens or remove its multicoating.

6. Camera strap. It is a mystery why camera cases are sold with thin leather straps since they tend to cut into the neck or shoulder. We prefer wide, comfortable camera straps, such as the OP/TECH strap. Hikers may prefer a special strap made to secure a camera close to the body.

7. Camera bag. Whatever your personal preference, a camera bag should be waterproof and roomy enough so you can see and easily remove all your equipment while keeping items in secure, separate compartments. The bag should be compact enough to stow under an airplane seat, since you will not want to check it. Belly packs are handy for daily outings, even if they are too small for all your gear. They are easy to carry and reduce the likelihood of loss, or the risk of theft. Many people like photographer's vests, which are fitted with pockets and zippered compartments to hold all kinds of equipment.

8. Tripod. A tripod is a must for night photography, interior shots, and other low-light situations where sharpness is critical. The challenge is to find one that is small enough to fit into a suitcase, yet sturdy enough to be steady when fully extended. Do not bother with tabletop models, which are not much lighter than full-size tripods and not nearly as useful. Also, we strongly recommend a medium-size ball-head for easy maneuverability. We recommend the Gitzo 620 with the Slik medium ball-head.

9. Notebook and pens. Take along writing equipment for recording photo information and names and addresses of people and places—which you may need for captions in albums or to review your technique. Also, a permanent marker, such as Sanford's Sharpie, simplifies writing directly on film canisters.

10. Soft cloth. A washcloth or other small terry cloth is invaluable for wiping dust or moisture off your camera and for shielding it from the elements.

11. Cable release. A must for time exposures, such as those taken at night, a cable release should be 12 to 18 inches (30 to 40 cm) long.

12. Hand-held meter. A spot meter is the best gauge for exposure, though it is more expensive than a standard hand-held meter. Not an absolute necessity, a spot meter is handy as a check against your camera's built-in metering system and as a back-up in case your SLR has metering problems.

13. Flashlight. A small Maglite or a similar type of flashlight has many uses for the traveling shutterbug, especially for reading controls and finding items in your camera bag during night photography and in dim interiors. Remember to bring extra batteries.

A lens shade was essential to reduce flare and extraneous light in this picture of a Dutch tulip field at sunset. Keep a lens shade on all lenses at all times. For a point-and-shoot camera, block flare by hand while looking through your lens.

TAKING CARE OF GEAR

During a journey replacement items may be hard to find, especially in such remote places as Mali, where shepherds and their flocks still cross the Niger River by canoe. It is prudent to bring extra batteries, protect gear from moisture and dirt, and clean equipment regularly.

Few of us remember to think about protecting and maintaining equipment, especially when we are in transit and having a good time. Still, knowing that camera gear takes quite a beating during travel, and considering how disappointed you would be if your equipment did not perform as expected, it is worthwhile to take some simple precautions, as well as to establish a maintenance routine while on the road.

Start your journey with everything in good working order. Before you leave, have your camera and lenses checked and cleaned professionally. Make any repairs that are needed, or invest in new items to replace those not worth fixing. During the trip, preferably at the end of each day, take a few minutes to check your gear and to restore it to tip-top condition.

The following suggestions should be helpful:
1. Camera. Protect your camera against humidity and moisture by keeping it in a plastic bag when not in use. A leather case offers good protection against bumps and knocks while a camera is in transit, but it is a cumbersome nuisance when you want to take pictures. Carry your camera in a small bag or belly pack, with a wide strap—but not in a case—so it is ready to use in an instant.

    Clean your camera every few days. If you are traveling in a sandy or dusty environment, it is best to clean it daily. Sand can cause camera mechanisms to jam, and if sand enters the camera's interior, it will scratch the film. Loosen surface dirt with a camel's hair brush, blow off dust with a rubber bulb blower, and wipe away grease or grime with a soft cloth. With SLRs, remove the lens and blow out the interior of the camera body. Then, with no film in the camera, open the back and blow it out.

2. Lenses. Protect all your lenses with skylight filters, sun-shades, and lens caps. You may want to carry your lenses in their leather packing cases, if space permits. Cleaning lenses invariably causes some damage to their coating or surface. That is why it is so important to use a protective filter. In addition, blow out the barrels of all lenses regularly, at full extension, and wipe, as needed.

3. Film. Film needs protection from x-rays, heat, and humidity. Airport x-rays should not cause problems to film unless it will be repeatedly exposed. Lead-lined bags designed to protect film from x-rays are not used by most professionals. It is simpler to carry film without boxes in clear plastic bags and politely ask for a hand inspection. That avoids the x-rays altogether.

   Prolonged exposure to high temperatures or high humidity can damage film. Protect film by keeping it in sealed plastic bags, removing only the film that you will need for that day. Leave rolls of film that are exposed and unneeded in your hotel room. Never leave film in the sun or in a closed, glassed-in space, such as a car. For camping trips, keep an inexpensive cooler just for film.

4. Filters. To clean filters, first blow off loose particles, then breathe on the glass and rub it gently with lens tissue. Small scratches or spots on the filter will probably not affect the clarity of the image. Since filters are inexpensive, they should be replaced when they show too much wear and tear.

5. Flash unit. Place your electronic flash unit in a plastic bag when not in use to keep it dry and to prevent corrosion of contacts.

In desert locations, such as the ancient rock-carved city of Petra, Jordan, protect lenses with skylight filters, and remove sand or dust daily to prevent scratching of film or jamming of a sensitive lens or camera mechanism.

Knowing What to Expect

Before setting off on any journey, most of us collect information to help us prepare for the trip. We learn about the climate and weather, the food, the customs, and we memorize some phrases to help us get along.

In the same way, it is helpful to know what to expect photographically. We are not suggesting that you have a written agenda for pictures you plan to take, but if you are prepared, picture-taking will be more productive.

Answering the questions below will help you anticipate the images you may want to bring back and will guide you toward the equipment that will enable you to create them:

1. What are your likely subjects: people, natural beauty, wildlife, landscapes, architecture, and so forth? Which lenses are needed for these subjects?

2. What will the people's skin tones be? Will particular film, filter, or a flash unit help record these skin tones? Is the culture one in which people are likely to be cooperative or reluctant subjects? Which lenses will help capture people who may be unwilling subjects?

3. What will the weather and light be? Which film is best for the muted light of mist and rain or for the brilliant sun of the desert or tropics? Will a polarizer or other filters be needed?

4. What sort of landscape and environment are likely to be encountered? Which lenses are best for shooting wide open spaces? Thick woods? Rolling countryside? Sandy beaches? Or marshy fens?

It is also important to know how much time you will have for photography. If there are specific places and sights on your itinerary, you may need to plan ahead to get any special shots you have in mind. For example, we planned to take sunrise photographs at Bryce Canyon National Park, and we allotted time for two sunrise shoots, getting up well before dawn to get to the viewpoints on time. The first morning was too cloudy for the dramatic light we expected to see. The next day, after an uncertain start, we did get about fifteen minutes of the light we wanted.

Knowing what you expect enables you to make the time and also to get the cooperation of those traveling with you. And to avoid misunderstandings between you and your travel companions, it is better to make your photographic plans known in advance.

A traveler should anticipate light and weather conditions to increase the chances of bringing back the best possible photographs. Knowing that early morning mist fills Venice's Piazza San Marco, we arrived at dawn to find an empty plaza except for one graceful sweeper.

From our research we expected to experience the pleasure of sailing in feluccas on the Nile River, and we planned to photograph this activity.

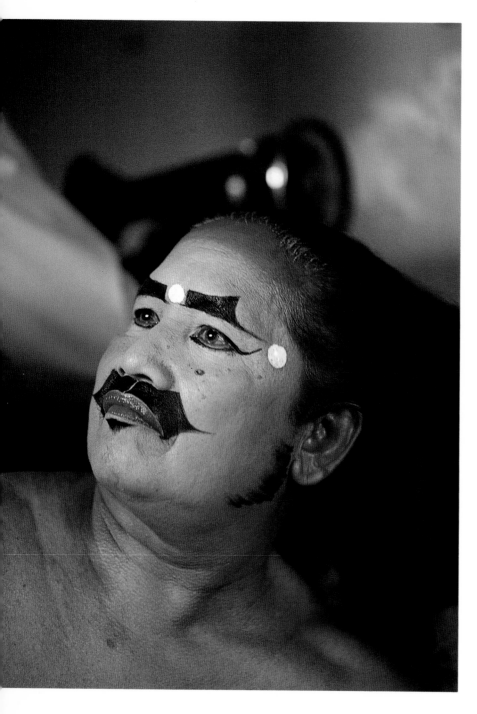

Practicing Before a Trip

In some ways photographing during travel is like competing in the Olympics: it may be the only chance you have to display your best skills by getting the pictures you want of a special scene or experience. But while no amateur athlete would dream of entering an Olympic event without extensive preparation, many amateur photographers do just that, leaving their once-in-a-lifetime opportunity to chance.

Of course, practicing your photography doesn't have to be as all-consuming a passion as rehearsing for an athletic event. In fact, the preparation can enrich your life at home, putting you in touch with previously undiscovered dimensions of your own locality. By practicing close to home, you will become more expert at seeing visual treasures everywhere.

Practicing also means attending to some technical matters like checking and testing your equipment and running at least one roll of the film you normally shoot. Activate your automatic features, such as autoexposure and autofocus, and shoot in a variety of situations to test the camera's accuracy. Keep notes on your shots so you can pinpoint any problems. Also, test the built-in flash mechanism for its performance—as fill-in light, in dim daylight, at night, and to stop motion.

Practicing helps you become familiar with the quirks of tools that may be new, borrowed, or have not been used for some time. The more you know about the behavior of your gear, the easier it will be for you to control its performance and to make it do your bidding when you're in the thick of it.

Rehearse your flash techniques, especially at close range, to get proper exposure when photographing people. This Balinese actor was backstage applying makeup before a performance.

Practice getting a sharp image while hand-holding a camera during a slow exposure before venturing into dimly lit markets like this one in Cairo, Egypt.

Experimenting Close to Home

Close to home, search for new ways to portray famous sights like the Capitol building in Washington, D.C., shown here framed by trees and behind a hedge of azaleas bordered by tulips.

There is much to photograph virtually in your own backyard, and perhaps there is no better place to develop your skills. You may even find subjects close to home that are a reasonable facsimile of those you plan to photograph during your travels.

You can practice your wildlife and nature photography, for example, at a local marsh or sanctuary. Natural enclaves provide opportunities for experimenting with composition, the use of natural light, and close-up equipment.

You don't have to go far out of town for vistas that enable you to prepare for far-off landscapes. Learn how to integrate foreground subjects with the background. Experiment with various lenses, especially those you have avoided. Begin to look at scenics in terms of their lines and shapes for interesting abstract arrangements. Develop pleasing ways to incorporate the sky in all kinds of weather and light.

You may discover interesting historic districts or churches nearby where you may hone your skills for photographing architecture. Street scenes and night shots can be rehearsed almost anywhere.

For portraits, family and friends of all ages could be asked to model, but consider other people you do not know personally, in local ethnic neighborhoods or in public places like markets, malls, and parks. County or craft fairs will give you a chance to try photographing people in candid or posed shots.

Practicing for a trip will not only refine your skills, but it will help you develop a new appreciation for your local surroundings.

OPPOSITE LEFT. *Before you leave on a trip, develop your skill in making the most of various light and weather conditions . This foggy cemetery was photographed during a weekend visit to Vermont.*

OPPOSITE RIGHT. *Learn to recognize beautiful light at the extremes of the day and practice working with it close to home. This winter sunrise scene was taken near a friend's home overlooking Buzzard's Bay in Massachusetts.*

3
The Language of Light

"All light is the best light."

ERNST HAAS, 1985

PAGES 58–59. *To capture the intimate sense of a travel experience requires an understanding of the qualities of light: its color, range of intensities, and varied directions. This riverside scene in Holland capitalizes on the warm, soft light of sunset.*

EXPOSING THE MOOD

No matter how much we have read about a place or how many pictures of it we have looked at, the feeling it conveys to us when we see it firsthand will be unique. Only a personal visit allows us to see, smell, hear, taste, and feel what a place is all about. As photographers, we try to translate those sensations into a visual mode. We want to capture the spirit, essence, or mood of a location as fully as we can, through pictorial means.

To communicate fluently through photography, we must first master the language of light, for available light is the raw material from which startling images are made. Light is the true and only subject of every snap of the shutter. While some manipulation is possible in the developing and printing process, the photograph is essentially made in the camera.

That is why learning to look at light with an analytic eye is a prerequisite for successful photography. Vital and fascinating, light casts its special quality over everything it envelops, suffusing it with moods of calm or excitement, sadness or gaiety, mystery or drama.

This chapter will illustrate how to make the most of different kinds of light throughout the day and night, and in all kinds of weather. With some appreciation of light, your travel photographs will not only capture a setting—they will also portray a palpable mood.

OPPOSITE. *Bright, high-contrast, late afternoon light, plus the exaggerated perspective of a 28mm lens, dramatizes this Colorado haystack.*

RIGHT. *Slight underexposure intensifies the pastel tones in this sunrise shot of Old Faithful in Yellowstone National Park in Wyoming.*

Sunrises and Sunsets

It is almost impossible to witness a sunrise or sunset and not be overwhelmed with feelings, as if the light itself had the power to control our mood. As we view the world, the low-angled rays at the extremes of the day cast long, dark shadows that make the most prosaic scene theatrical. The rays themselves often emerge through a partial cloud cover or through the foliage of trees, energizing a scene with such ethereal light that photographers are drawn to take pictures of it for its own sake.

The colors of the rising or setting sun are often spectacular and otherworldly. Sunrises tend toward soothing cool blues, pinks, greens, and mauves, while sunsets lean toward fiery oranges and reds. The sky, the landscape, and the most ordinary street scenes are bathed in a vibrant glow. Look for such light wherever you travel, and take advantage of it when you find it.

As for photographs of sunrises and sunsets, these require some special adjustments. The most common mistake photographers make is metering or aiming directly into the sun. Since the sun is much brighter than its surroundings, shooting at the meter reading for the sun underexposes the rest of the frame, leaving the sun in a sea of darkness, not what most people have in mind when they photograph sunrises or sunsets.

The simplest way to avoid this problem is to change the metering procedure and allow some overexposure of the sun. Those with SLRs should meter both the sun and its surroundings—the clouds, the ocean, the beach. Then, choose an exposure in between the two readings. Finally, bracket to ensure at least one "best" exposure. Those with automatic cameras should meter by turning away from the sun and then locking in that reading before composing to shoot toward the sun.

TOP. *A zoom lens set at 250mm enlarges the sun as it sinks into the Indian Ocean. Overexposing half a stop from a meter reading of the sky brightens colors.*

ABOVE. *To enrich colors and highlight the rays of a sunset obscured by a cloud, meter the cloud and underexpose one stop. Scenes like this one off the coast of Indonesia can be found around the world.*

In the Midday Sun

While the extremes of the day may provide the most interesting light for photographs, travelers take most of their pictures in the middle of the day. Contrary to popular belief, bright midday light is the most difficult to control photographically.

The midday sun tends to be very intense, especially in summer, and can easily bleach out colors. The challenge, then, is to keep the colors lush while retaining the charged quality of the light. With slide film, this can be done by underexposing in 1/2 stop intervals, up to 1 1/2 f-stops. Otherwise, try a polarizing filter to reduce glare and eliminate reflections. The true colors of the sky, foliage, water, and various other surfaces can then show through.

Another problem with the midday sun is that it creates harsh contrasts between areas in sun and shadow. Such high-contrast situations are very hard to expose properly, since either the bright or shadowed areas will tend to lose detail, especially with slide film.

One way to get out of this dilemma is to eliminate either of the extremes from the picture frame: shoot either the sunny *or* the shady side of the street. Then exposure can be based on the bright or the shadowed area, but not both. A second solution entails juxtaposing the two extremes in a graphic combination so one serves as a backdrop or frame for the other. For example, an archway in shade can frame the building or street glimpsed through it. Or brightly lit flowers can be set against shadowy shrubs. In these instances, expose for the bright areas so they retain their rich colors, and allow the shadows to go black.

A special word of caution needs to be added about photographing people in the midday sun. The strong, overhead light casts downward shadows, which we may not notice while we are photographing, but which become all too visible

Deep shadows cast by the midday sun frame the golden wheat and muted grasses in this Colorado landscape.

when we look at the results. Also, people tend to squint and squirm in bright sunlight.

If at all possible, photograph people in the shade, where the light will be more uniform. If the sun is unavoidable, have your subject face away from the sun, not toward it, and meter the face at close range, within 1 foot. This backlit arrangement may overexpose the background, but the person's features will be natural.

Silhouettes and Shadows

"If you have a lemon, make lemonade," an old saying advises. That same homespun philosophy of turning liabilities into assets can be applied to photography. What appear to be problems—the very intense midday light or the strongly directional light of sunrise and sunset—can often become their own solutions through creative thinking and seeing.

One approach is to have fun with silhouettes. Silhouettes are simply photographs in which the foreground subject is severely underexposed, while the background is in good exposure. Silhouettes often add interest to an otherwise bland composition. Think of trees silhouetted against the sky, or a sculpture silhouetted against a cityscape. To be effective, the silhouette should be a well-defined form or shape, so it serves as a visual point of reference. The background should be rich in color or texture, so it acts as a counterpoint to the stark foreground silhouette.

Another creative possibility is to incorporate shadows into the photographic composition. Shadows can be very graphic visual elements. If you look at a scene in terms of the play of shadow and sunlight, you may discover an evocative or startling relationship. Focusing on the graphic components, regardless of what the other "subjects" of the photograph might be, helps feature the purely formal aspects of a scene.

Exposure in such formal, abstract portrayals of travel destinations should be based on the qualities of the light and the mood you wish to emphasize. Underexposure will appear more dramatic or sinister. Overexposure will bring out softer, more delicate qualities.

TOP. *The dark triangular silhouettes of these slopes in Idaho are balanced by the textured gravel in the foreground and the puffy clouds.*

LEFT. *Two whimsical shadows—the larger cast by Delicate Arch, the smaller by the photographer—present an offbeat interpretation of Arches National Park in Utah.*

Reflections

In a sense reflections are illusions that can be documented. We said earlier that photography's raw material is light. That light can come directly from a source, such as the sun, a streetlight, or a candle. Or, as is much more common, it can be light that is reflected from the surfaces of all the objects in the world. While many of the photographs we take are of "reflections," there are some highly reflective surfaces that offer the traveling photographer new visual dimensions.

Water is a favorite reflective surface to photograph. Still water is a glassy double of the world. As ripples or waves break the water's surface, unexpected shapes, colors, and patterns emerge. Both a faithful likeness of water and a distorted image offer dramatic possibilities for portraying locations we are viewing for the first time or exploring more fully. Before snapping the shutter, take some time to watch moment-by-moment changes in the water's surface, and be prepared to capture the fleeting image that means the most to you.

The glass of windows and of the walls of skyscrapers, the sheen of a rain-slicked street, a mirror on a hotel wall all reflect light in intriguing, unexpected ways that warrant a photographer's attention.

A few caveats about photographing reflections:
1. Reflections can occur together with extraneous light, which reduces their richness and clarity. A polarizing filter can remove as much or as little of this unwanted light as is needed, and underexposure can deepen color intensity.
2. If a photograph depicts a reflection and its source—a land form, a boat, a face—look carefully to determine the point of focus. In general, focus on the "real thing" rather than on the reflection. Today's autofocus cameras may have difficulty with such reflections.
3. Symmetry works with most reflections. Be daring, if you wish, by trying some asymmetrical compositions, but when in doubt, fall back on a familiar composition.

The marvel of reflections in still water, here azaleas in a luminous pond in South Carolina's Middleton Gardens, convey a magical atmosphere.

A silhouette of a single tree on the shore of Holland's River Vecht radiates sunset light reflected in the water.

EXCITEMENT AFTER DARK

Perhaps the most neglected opportunities for the travel photographer occur after dark. Nighttime can convey the mood of a place in a new way, and since many "sights" are closed in the evenings, there is time to explore a place in an unhurried way.

Nighttime photography is easier than most people realize, because it has nothing to do with using flash equipment and everything to do with the way film works. Film has the capacity to accumulate light. When we take an exposure, we open the camera's aperture for a period of time, allowing light to enter and strike the film.

As long as there is some light, even a very little bit, it is possible to create an image. The sky provides a rich backdrop for any number of subjects, its colors ranging from a deep azure just after sunset to the pitch black of midnight. Well-exposed photographs can be made simply by keeping the shutter open for a longer period of time. Trying to take such pictures using flash is a waste of film and effort since the flash's small burst of light cannot illuminate distant or panoramic scenes.

Think of all the kinds of light one can find after dark: moonlight and starlight, street lamps, a car's headlights and taillights, storefront displays, floodlights, traffic lights, amusement park lights, and so much more. Another dimension is added to your nighttime photographs if the subjects are in motion. Moving lights register on film as streaks or bands. As these colorful ribbons of light swirl before the camera, the startling effects are unlimited.

Part of the fun of nighttime photography is not knowing exactly what the pictures will look like. Since the image is a kind of illusion, the photographer's role is to experiment. The results are a surprise gift to ourselves with the package to be opened when we get back home.

A nighttime skyline, like this one of Manhattan, is an easy and predictable subject. Just meter the sky, and underexpose to saturate colors and to deepen the black.

In the Still of the Night

The glow of floodlights softened by misty rain set off a cross at the Duomo in Florence. With uniform light, a slight underexposure on the cross did not obscure the background. A small aperture maximized sharpness at a 6-second exposure.

There is magic in the night, and still film is uniquely suited to making the magic visible. The main accessory needed for night photography is a tripod, which will keep the camera absolutely steady during time exposures. Begin your nighttime shooting with such stationary subjects as floodlit monuments, street scenes, or skylines.

The procedure is quite simple:
1. Set the camera on a tripod and compose carefully.
2. Assuming that you are working at some distance from the subject, with the focus ring set at infinity, select an aperture between f/5.6 and f/8 for sharpness.
3. With your camera set for autoexposure, take a series of bracketed shots by turning the compensation dial from +1 and +2 to -1. Be prepared for exposures that may range from 5 seconds to 1 minute, depending on the brightness of the subject. With SLRs, meter the scene, preferably with a spot meter, aiming at those dark areas that you want to expose with some clarity.

An interesting effect of using a slow shutter speed is that moving objects can vanish or turn to pale ghosts. People walking quickly across the picture frame will effectively disappear, so you need not wait until they are "out of the way."

Prepare some tests at home before your trip if you are interested in trying your hand at night photography. Then, during your travels, work within a range of settings that give you results you like. Continue to bracket liberally because night lights are quite variable and hard to gauge accurately.

Think carefully about the film you wish to use with each light source. Remember that films are balanced for a particular light. However, fascinating effects can be created by deliberately mismatching the film and the light source. Daylight film used to photograph fluorescent light gives a green appearance; incandescent light looks yellow or orange; and tungsten film transforms a dull, grayish sunset sky to azure blue.

Lights in Motion

Night photography comes alive when the light source is in motion. A car's headlights and taillights on city streets or country roads, neon lights blinking wildly, carousels and other rides in amusement parks all make excellent subjects for night photography.

With a slow shutter speed, moving lights will register as streaks or swirls. A tripod will keep the camera absolutely steady during long exposures. Use a cable release with the shutter set at the B or bulb setting and a stopwatch or second hand to keep track of exposure times. Since exact exposure levels are very hard to gauge, experiment with at least five or six shots for each scene.

Once you have mastered the basics, be imaginative. Try taking the camera off the tripod, and during exposure pan a moving subject by following it in your viewfinder. Select a single horse on a carousel, for example, and keep it in your frame as it moves from left to right. Or try zooming in or out during exposure for some really dazzling effects. Do not worry about perfect focus or absolute clarity. You are striving to capture impressionistic images portraying motion.

The swirl of car lights passing the Flatiron Building in New York City was caught from another skyscraper, using a 10 second exposure. While a series of pictures was taken at different exposure times, the same small aperture was used to get a successful image.

Since there is no way to predict what a particular fireworks display will look like, set your camera for a wide perspective. These fireworks were shot during the Desert Storm victory celebration in New York City.

Fireworks and Lightning

The nighttime sky—a dark backdrop for scenes of moonlit mystery, slow movement of stars and planets, irregular crackling of lightning, and glittering explosions of fireworks—has captured the imagination of generations of photographers. Travel often takes us to places where these natural and man-made celestial events take on added meaning, either because they are visible as never before, or simply because we have the time to appreciate them.

The techniques for photographing the night sky are similar to those already discussed. There are, however, some further considerations:

1. Under optimum weather conditions pictures of the moon and stars require very long exposures, ranging from several minutes to half an hour, but a bright moon can be photographed at a fraction of a second. A telephoto lens helps enlarge the image of the moon, but be sure to include part of the landscape or cityscape to provide a context and scale. The moon appears largest at the horizon as it rises. The exact time and location of the moonrise are generally available in local newspapers.

2. While lightning never strikes twice, you will probably need more than one strike for an effective photograph. Double or multiple exposures will give you that opportunity.

3. To show the full panorama of a fireworks display, use a wide-angle lens. To capture just the bursts of light in the sky, a moderate telephoto lens—85mm to 135mm—works best.

TOP. *To record a nighttime storm over Central Park in New York City, the aperture was kept open during three consecutive lightning strikes.*

ABOVE. *A 3-second exposure caught multiple bursts of a colorful fireworks finale at Florida's Disneyworld.*

WHATEVER THE WEATHER

There are photographic gems to be found in less than ideal weather. In fact, we do not cancel our outdoor workshops because of rain. Once, during a photography class in New York's Central Park, a summer thunderstorm burst upon us. Our students's first reaction was to pack up and leave the park. But we persuaded them to retreat to the shelter of a nearby tunnel. From this safe haven, the class produced the best photographs of the course.

Not only can your vacation photographs be salvaged, but you can actually discover unexpected beauty as you learn to work in "foul" weather. Clouds and rain seem to play no part in most people's photographic—or vacation—plans. Yet the images you can create in inclement weather will convey the mood of the setting in a new way.

There are a few precautions to take:
1. Protect your gear. Keep your camera wrapped in a plastic bag until you are ready to shoot. Simply place the bag around the lens, securing it to the barrel with a rubber band. Leave an opening at the front, extending a bit beyond the edge of the lens. A lens shade and skylight filter will protect the lens itself.
2. Set your camera on a tripod. You will probably be shooting at slow shutter speeds because of low light or to emphasize the movement of raindrops or snowflakes.
3. Dress comfortably. The elements will not bother you if you wear sturdy, watertight shoes and a waterproof slicker. Hats, gloves, thick socks, and boots will help you stay warm.

We have made such converts of some of our students that they now look disappointed when the sun is shining!

PAGES 72–73. *A threatening sky, pierced by flashes of light that dazzled the seagull and the water, provided the right conditions for this wide-angle shot of San Francisco Bay taken from the ferry to Sausalito.*

Hazy Days

The light of a hazy, cloudy day is, in many ways, ideal for travel and for photography. The light is easier on the eyes for sightseeing, and the sights themselves are spared unwanted reflections and distracting highlights by a cloud cover that filters, softens, and diffuses the light of the sun. This is wonderful light for scenics and panoramas: landscapes are richer in color because there is no bright sun to bleach them out. City scenes also benefit from the color saturation made possible by the even, diffused light.

Under these conditions it is best to include as little of the sky as possible, or none at all. Because an overcast sky lacks color, it appears in photographs as a bland expanse of white. Before you release the shutter, check the composition and framing carefully. If you see too much sky, just tip the camera down slightly, change from a vertical to a horizontal format, or turn the camera slightly to the left or right so that a tree or other object can camouflage the sky.

Vignettes and details, which eliminate the sky, are especially well suited to this muted light. Architectural forms can be cleanly portrayed, without the marring presence of harsh shadows. Nature close-ups, flowers, and gardens also photograph beautifully, with enhanced colors and textures. Portraits also work well in the light of a cloudy day, because people's faces are spared the downcast shadows prevalent in bright sun.

OPPOSITE. *On an overcast day in autumn, hazy light saturates and delineates the warm colors of this Vermont scene.*

RIGHT. *Uniform, hazy light—common at Keukenhof Gardens in Holland—minimizes shadows and brings out details, whether you are photographing people or scenery.*

ABOVE. *While waiting for these Ghanaian women to reach the misty part of the beach, the photographer metered the mist and underexposed half a stop to create silhouettes.*

RIGHT. *As morning mist rises in the Colorado Rockies, the sun makes it glow. We metered the dark area of the mist and shot at the meter reading to keep the bright areas white.*

OPPOSITE. *Rainy days often reveal unusual images, like this one of a tribesman in rural Papua, New Guinea, who walked into view with his umbrella on his way home after a ceremonial "sing-sing."*

Fog, Mist, and Rain

There are travel photographers so enthralled by the romantic, mysterious aura of fog and mist that they seek out these elements in places like Ireland or England. And since fog and mist are not usual conditions, one should not waste the chance to photograph them when they occur.

Mist is most readily found in the earliest hour of the day in coastal or highly vegetated areas. The mist rises immediately after sunrise and floats weightlessly just above the ground for about half an hour. Those who want the opportunity to photograph mist will have to venture out at daybreak, for as soon as the sun has warmed the air sufficiently, the mist vanishes. Mist is also likely to be found in a hot, humid environment right after a rainstorm. Again, this mist is short-lived, though it tends to appear in the more civilized late afternoon

Fog is a common coastal and mountain phenomenon, shrouding the scene in a milky white veil. Bits and pieces of a landscape peer through the fog, first in one place and then in another, as the fog meanders along its wispy path.

Both fog and mist retain their pristine whiteness when photographed slightly overexposed by 1/2 stop above the meter reading.

A gentle rain may not be something to wish for while traveling, but it should not be viewed as a deterrent to good photography. Evocative images can be captured right through such rain. With a slow shutter speed, the rain will register as thin lines or streaks, through which a charming village or country road can be glimpsed. The slick sheen of rocks and city streets on a rainy day gives them a special radiance. And droplets of rain on flowers and foliage are so desirable in photographs that some professionals carry misters just to create this effect.

Storms and Rainbows

The edge of a storm cloud in Colorado heightens the wondrous sunset colors. To saturate those colors, meter the middle tones in the clouds and underexpose.

Nature's high drama, thunderstorms, are recurring phenomena in mountainous or tropical areas. As in a play they usually occur in several predictable acts, all prime photographic targets.

Act one consists of preparation for the storm. A gathering of thunderclouds rolls over the landscape. Accompanied by a rumble of thunder, the approaching clouds gradually block out sun and light. The counterpoint of the sun, which struggles to remain visible, and the clouds, which are determined to overpower the sun's rays, produces a wonderful visual tension, especially with sun showers. Capture the light behind the rim of the clouds by metering the landscape, not the sky.

In act two, the landscape darkens and shimmers with a silvery sheen. Flashes of lightning may be seen in the distance, and the sight, sound, and smell of a downpour fulfill the promise of the storm. Again, meter and expose for the landscape to keep the thunderclouds dark and ominous.

A storm is exciting to photograph from a position of safety and comfort. At a distance, it can be photographed, with few precautions, using a telephoto lens. If the storm is without lightning, a large, sturdy umbrella held by a companion can keep you photographing dryly and happily for a long time. Otherwise, find a refuge—a car, a porch, a doorway—from which you can observe and photograph as the drama continues to unfold.

Act three is the finale. As the drenching rain tapers to a few droplets, the refracted light of the reemerging sun may emblazon the sky with a rainbow. This is when photographers become children, chasing rainbows with delight and abandon. To increase your chances of catching a rainbow, meter the background and underexpose by 1/2 and 1 full f-stop to saturate the rainbow's colors.

And if thunderstorms are not your cup of tea, look for rainbows in the mists of waterfalls—and remember to underexpose—and in oil slicks, which need no special photographic considerations.

LEFT. *To catch a rainbow, a photographer must work quickly and knowledgeably. Meter the sky and underexpose one stop. Polarize to intensify colors.*

ABOVE. *A storm is visible from a distance on the wide open spaces of a Colorado high plateau. To darken and concentrate the area of downpour, meter the clouds and underexpose up to one and one-half stops. The added contrast will portray more vividly any lightning that occurs.*

Snow scenes, such as this one, taken at the New York Botanical Garden, will look white if the meter reading is taken off something neutral grey, like the trees.

Snow and Ice

Trips to colder climates are popular for many travelers, not just for winter sports and recreation, but for appreciating the pristine beauty of glaciers and natural surroundings. And in these regions the photo opportunities are endless.

Whatever the subject, if it is in snow, it will require some photographic adaptations. The main challenge is to keep the snow white. In dull light, this is best achieved through some overexposure from the meter reading. In very bright sunshine, meter something that is not white and lock in that reading to avoid the effects of glare.

Films differ in the way they render the color of snow. Slide films using E-6 processing, such as Ektachrome and Fuji-chrome, tend to turn snow bluish, while Kodachrome films veer toward a pinkish hue. To compensate for these color shifts, use the appropriate color correction filters, as shown in the appendix.

Falling snow is not just fun to experience but fun to capture on film. If you're looking for that perfect Christmas card picture, try shooting a scene as it is being blanketed by snow. To show the slow floating movement of snowflakes, use a shutter speed of 1/4 of a second to 1 second. The streaks of a faster snowfall are made with shutter speeds of 1/30 of a second to 1/8 of a second. Or, if you prefer suspending the flakes in midair, shoot at a shutter speed of 1/60 of a second or faster.

Photographing ice on a lake or skating pond involves essentially the same techniques as for shooting snow. Avoid metering areas of glare but include them in your photograph because their brightness often adds to the image.

Take some precautions when photographing in cold weather. Keep your camera dry and warm when not in use, perhaps carrying it inside your jacket. Because batteries lose power quickly in the cold, it is prudent to bring along spares. Wear thin leather gloves to grip and hold metal gear, such as a tripod. Most important, keep your head, hands, and feet warm if you plan to photograph in frigid conditions.

The Harvard Glacier, in Prince William Sound, Alaska, was underexposed one-half stop to saturate its blue color. It was then shot at a fast shutter speed to capture the "calving" phenomenon, as chunks of the glacier fall off into the water.

4
Creating a Personal Style

*"Of what use are lens and light
to those who lack mind and sight."*

LATIN INSCRIPTION, 1589

ORGANIZING CHAOS

Photography is often thought of as an objective medium, one that records what we see. In a way, of course, that is true. But it is not that simple. The world we see is a fairly chaotic place. When we travel, our eyes take in images from every direction. Some things go by so quickly, or we pass them by so casually, that we don't consider them worth photographing. Other sights attract our attention, but when we try to photograph them we have difficulty portraying exactly what appealed to us.

The very act of picking up a camera and pointing it in a certain direction indicates selectivity. As photographers, we look at the world through the filter of our own preferences and personalities. We see not only what is but what might be. We look at randomness and project ourselves through the meanings we find and the order we impose. We decide with every frame what is worth portraying. Our objective as photographers is to choose carefully and deliberately.

To become better at selecting exactly what to capture on film, thereby expressing our individual vision and developing a personal style, requires a mastery of the language of composition and color, for these are the unifying elements that organize our vision. If we think about these fundamentals—discussed in this chapter—before we snap a picture, our photographs will be more satisfying to us because they will reveal our true intentions.

PAGES 82–83. *Knowing what you wish to feature in an image is basic to the development of a personal style. This pastoral landscape combines typical elements seen in northern Holland—the lines of a meandering stream, a perfectly flat horizon, the distinctive shape of a windmill, and the repeating forms of three grazing horses.*

ABOVE. *The unexpected addition of a barbed wire cross organizes this portrayal of the San Xavier Mission and its cemetery outside Tucson, Arizona.*

OPPOSITE. *An ordinary lake view in upstate New York is dramatized through its bold symmetry, simple shapes, and limited palate.*

A simple arrangement of sunwashed architec-
tural forms conveys the essence of the
Greek island of Thíra (formerly
Santorini).

A human figure becomes part of an abstract
design of colors and shapes taken on a
street in Ghana.

Clarity and Simplicity

Clarity of purpose puts you in control and helps you succeed in taking the pictures you really want. Travelers often photograph too quickly, and the resulting photographs are inadequately composed and disjointed.

Here are some pointers to help you control your picture-taking:

1. Be purposeful. If you have trouble identifying your intent, try finishing this sentence: "What I want to show is . . ." Knowing your purpose helps distill each image to its essence. Then figure out how best to fill the frame to show only what is important to you. You may need to use a certain lens, or to move closer, or to change your angle to create the image in your mind's eye.
2. Examine your image carefully. Once you understand your purpose, force yourself to see what you may otherwise overlook. Look to the edges and corners of each frame and eliminate anything distracting or unnecessary. If the neat arrangement of mangoes is what interests you, do not include the oranges and apples as well. There is no reason to show the buses and cars on a street in front of a cathedral. If you intend to show the beauty of a beach at sunset, you will want to exclude the basket overflowing with garbage. And notice if a tree or telephone pole appears to be growing from a travel companion's head.
3. Less is more. Simplify your composition by moving closer, moving to the side, or selecting a different lens. These small steps pay off in tighter, more pleasing compositional arrangements.
4. Look beyond the subject. A lovely picture is often spoiled by distractions in the background. The background is an integral part of every photograph, one that can and should add to your purpose. If a well-defined background serves your intent, by all means keep it sharp and well exposed. But a distracting, confusing, or unnecessary background

should be scrupulously eliminated by being blurred out, or by changing the camera's perspective, or by taking advantage of contrasting light.

ABOVE. *In Ghana a display of mangoes in a market inspired this simple composition based on repeated shapes and contrasting colors.*

PAGES 88–89. *In this personal composition we wished to show the shape and scale of the Great Sand Dunes in Colorado by homing in on a section of the dunes that were defined by light and shadow. Then we waited for people to walk to the right spot.*

PAGE 89. *The arch of a massive concrete hydroelectric dam high in the Swiss Alps gracefully curves across the picture frame.*

The converging lines of a canal, the form of a gondola, and the shape of a bridge capture the spirit of Venice.

Lines, Shapes, and Forms

Our tendency is to look at the world as a series of objects that we can name and identify. To be fluent in the language of photography, we need to translate these "things" into pictorial elements—lines, shapes, and forms—and then to fill the frame in a way that creates harmony and balance.

Lines appear in a photograph wherever two edges meet: a building and the sky, a sidewalk and a gutter, one side of a sand dune and another, a field and a road. Photographers can increase the impact of an image by making the lines point smoothly and gracefully in the right direction.

Lines draw the viewer's eye from one part of the plane to another. Horizontal and vertical lines can reinforce a sense of flatness, while diagonals can create an illusion of depth. S- and C-curves add a dynamic quality to still photographs.

Everything has a shape, and photographers learn to strip away the subjective meaning of each object and view it as a form filling the space of the picture frame. In doing this, we learn that certain shapes work well together, while others are not harmonious. For example, curves and circles may be a pleasing combination, unlike rectangles and radiating lines. While there are no definite rules, the point is to begin thinking about such issues to activate your own aesthetic preferences.

Natural forms can also create shapes within the picture frame. The most common one is the sky. Inexperienced photographers rarely think of the sky as a shape, but it is just that, whether as a thin or wide rectangle above a flat horizon, an undulating shape over a hilly terrain, or a jagged, hard-edged abstraction around a skyline. Whatever its shape, the sky will play a visible role in the final image and should be given thought.

The shape of shadows, which often become blocks of black in a photograph, should be integrated into the whole. Shadows cast into a bright area also become visible shapes.

Instead of ignoring them, incorporate them imaginatively into your composition.

Finally, shapes are created by the way the photographer frames and focuses a subject. The frame defines and limits the visible world in such a way that new forms emerge, based only on the photographer's ability to see things not as they are, but as they might be. Similarly, selective focusing causes parts of the image to blur. The blurs become separate shapes that isolate a foreground object from a backdrop.

The simple shapes of land and sky are overlaid with the converging lines of a daffodil field and the amorphous forms of puffy clouds in this Dutch scenic.

Death Valley, California is reduced to its basic forms—dune and sky—in this carefully balanced composition.

A row of gnarled trees and colorful bands of flowers press together in this telephoto shot taken in Keukenhof Gardens in Holland.

Patterns and Rhythms

The repetition of forms and lines creates patterns and rhythms. Such repetition is part of the language of photography, giving order and coherence to the randomness of the world we see.

Some patterns are easy to recognize and depict. Think of a coastline strewn with briny stones. There is something evocative and soothing about seeing many of those stones as they recede along the shore. Or think of a city or village street with similar houses in a row. They need to be identical to engage us with their repeated doorways, windows, and steps.

Other patterns are not so easy to recognize. These tend to be patterns within the larger whole, which we are accustomed to seeing as a unit. For example, if we enter a church, we may experience the interior as a single vision, or as an interplay of stained-glass windows, stone columns, and wooden pews. If we look at these elements more individually, we can begin to see rhythms at play: the columns, pews, or chandeliers can be viewed as a repeated series of individual forms and can be visually organized to show a more interesting relationship.

As your eye becomes keener, you will find more possibilities for showing patterns and rhythms: trees in woods, steps in a park, boats near docks, produce in markets, and so much more.

The rhythmic flow of an ordinary staircase in Senegal becomes an evocative photograph because of the reflection on the wall, the light on the steps, and the asymmetrical composition.

Abstractions

The best photographs succeed as abstractions as well as documents. They combine visual and editorial content; they fuse aesthetics and meaning.

There are sights that appeal to us, however, as pure abstractions. Often we find these in the most unexpected places, and they would probably be of no interest to us except for their formal qualities. They are felicitous accidents upon which we stumble, visual delights that surprise and inspire us. Take, for example, an ordinary wall with peeling paint or with layers of old posters. With an imaginative eye, the wall could be a perfect abstract composition. The same may apply to faces of rocks in the desert, where the surface reveals swirling striations of sedimentation. Other examples include close-ups of textiles, tree barks, or oil slicks.

Not only do abstractions expand our visual repertoire, but as an added bonus for travelers, they often help start conversations with local people. Perhaps nothing is as fascinating to others as watching a stranger taking pictures of something whose importance no one can understand. More often than not, someone will wander over and ask what you are doing. This gives you a chance to chat, to let them look through your viewfinder, and to develop some rapport. After that, anything is possible. (We have been invited to tea, to family gatherings, and even to a wedding.)

We have found that local people are more at ease with us if we give them a chance to take the initiative. Doing something strange like shooting abstractions arouses their curiosity about us and allows them to be the ones to take the first step.

TOP. *A detail of peeling paint on the bow of a boat in Bass Harbor, Maine, is an abstract study in color and shape.*

LEFT. *A typical street scene in Dakar, Senegal, was composed for its abstract values rather than as a documentary cityscape.*

A stained-glass church window in Mykonos casts a
red reflection onto a windowsill to create blocks
of color reminiscent of a painting by Mondrian.

THE MEANING OF COLOR

The world is filled with an endless spectrum of color, and the human eye is capable of distinguishing thousands of shades. Most of us, however, are inured to the reality of color in our everyday lives. Travel primes us to notice color anew, and photography pushes us to think more deliberately about color

Colors have taken on rich meanings because of their associations with places, emotions, and cultures. Specific locations

ABOVE. *A cacophony of vivid pastel colors, from the painted stucco houses to their reflections in a nearby canal, are typical visual delights of Burano, Italy.*

RIGHT. *The crimson ceremonial robes of this Japanese gentleman, framed against an equally brilliant red sun umbrella, form a photograph defined by a single dominant color.*

around the world can often be recognized by the distinct coloration of their natural environment. The soil may be black or clay red, the sands may be powder white or coral pink, the rocks may be the cool gray of granite or the chalky white of limestone.

Even the color of the sky, the water, and the vegetation can be linked to a place. The aquamarine sky of Tuscany is quite different from the misty gray of England's, or the brilliant blue sky of the Negev desert. And the shade of green seen in a rice field is unique among crops.

Part of what we want to develop as travel photographers is a special sensitivity to the colors we find in each location. In addition, however, we need to understand the emotional and cultural meanings of colors, many of which function on an unconscious level. Psychologists have studied the effects of color on emotions, and their findings have been used by designers and decorators as a hidden code with which to communicate. Cool colors, such as pale blue, for example, tend to promote calm and tranquility, whereas reds, magentas, and hot pinks are linked with excitement.

Different cultures assign different meanings to colors. In the West, the color associated with death is black, but in India it is white. Blue and green represent good fortune in Islamic communities and, as a result, many house interiors are painted with these colors. Knowing the cultural significance of colors will enhance your ability to use them appropriately in pictures.

On a purely pictorial level, colors also play an important role in the appeal of our photographs. Whether quietly monochromatic or loud and gaudy, colors in our photographs help create a personal aesthetic style.

The neutral tones of the sky, the beach, and the catamaran set off the bright red sail.

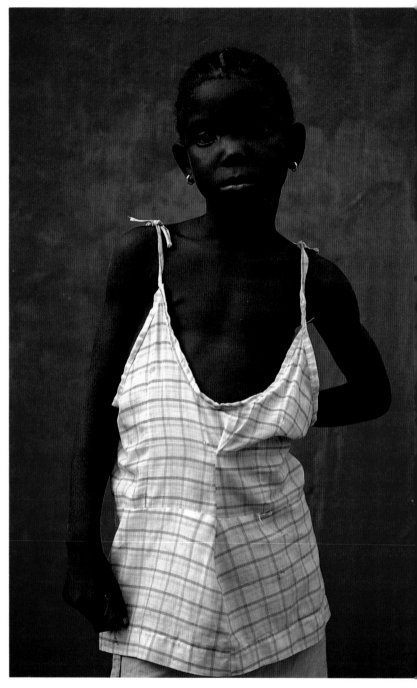

ABOVE. *During the festival of Pongal in southern India, women create intricate good luck designs at their doorsteps using colorful chalk powders, shown here in the shade of a market stall.*

RIGHT. *To take this portrait of a young girl in Ghana, we asked her to stand in front of a wall painted a deep rust color.*

OPPOSITE. *A simple composition featuring colors, shapes, and lines is actually details of a house in Jodhpur, India.*

Vivid Colors

Vivid colors are like the sounds of a trumpet. They demand—and get—your immediate attention. They include the pure reds, bright greens, royal blues, or iridescent pinks that come to us fully saturated, undiminished by traces of black or white. While they are easy to see, they are not simple to photograph.

To understand how to photograph vivid colors, we must consider how light affects the way these colors will record on film. Bright sunlight is often an enemy to vivid colors, adding so much white light to these hues that they become diluted beyond recognition. This is particularly a problem with slide film, which has less latitude than negative film. Use a polarizing filter with slide film in intense light, and, if necessary, underexpose up to 1/2 to 1 full f-stop.

Your choice of film can also make a difference in how vivid colors are rendered. Brilliant colors in bright light hold up best with Ektachrome, Kodachrome, and Fujichrome 100 films. Diffused light, found in shaded areas or on cloudy days, is much kinder to vivid colors, leaving them as they actually appear, especially when shot with Fujichrome Velvia film.

Since vivid colors tend to demand our attention—visually, they may cause a "flickering" sensation—choose one color as the dominant one for any image, and allow the other bright colors to play supporting roles. This is easiest to accomplish in locations with broad expanses of a single color: landscapes where green dominates, fields and gardens with beds of one kind of flower, towns where houses are the same color. If several vivid colors are combined, be sure to keep the composition simple through a neat arrangement of lines or shapes and by eliminating or blurring out any background distractions.

Muted Colors

Muted colors are like the people we say have "character": they may look better in photographs than in reality, and they often have an evocative quality that gives them appeal for years to come.

These colors include pale pastels, grays of every shade, and whites and off-whites of every season. Because they are softer and more subtle than their bolder cousins, they are harder to notice and identify. But they combine well in a single composition and serve as versatile backgrounds for portraits. Soft colors are especially good for setting a mood of tranquility.

As with vivid colors, these muted tones also photograph best in diffused light. Kodachrome, Ektachrome EPX, and Fujichrome Velvia depict soft shades well, especially warm earth tones.

ABOVE. *The muted predawn colors at Bryce Canyon National Park in Utah require some overexposure to brighten the earthforms.*

RIGHT. *After sunset, the water of the river Vecht in Holland reflects the soft, tawny tones of the sky.*

A monochromatic photograph makes good use of the muted earth tones in this potter's workshop in Hebron, Israel.

5
Conveying a Sense of Place

"Each place, like a person, is unique,
with a style and a personality of
its own . . . the photographer has
only one job; to reveal that character
and communicate it to the viewer."

LANDSCAPES

If travel is motivated by one factor, it is the overwhelming desire to see and experience places different from those at home. People who have been bitten by the travel bug long to immerse themselves in a new natural or cultural environment. The sight of grand mountain vistas or sailboats slicing through water, the feel of mist along a coast or heat in a scorching desert, the vision of dark woods or quaint cottages are enough to conjure up an entire adventure fantasy.

As photographers, our greatest hope is to capture the essence of each location we visit, to bring back—for our own contemplation and to share with others—those scenes that will forever encompass what we saw and experienced. In this chapter, we will discuss some of the ways this can best be done, wherever your travels may take you. And while all location shots are, in a sense, landscapes, this chapter covers those that depict the grandeur of nature.

Landscape photography boasts a long and wonderful tradition. Many of the earliest photographs portrayed natural areas in the American West. While these were often taken by journeymen-photographers as part of a land survey, they became images that entered the popular imagination and influenced governmental decisions to preserve the large tracts of unspoiled natural beauty that became our national parks.

As we photograph landscapes today, we can still feel the freshness of discovery if we let a sense of awe overwhelm us. Without an emotional involvement, our photographs may lose their luster; with it, we can hope to convey the magic and majesty of all we survey.

The most difficult quality to capture in landscapes is each

PAGES 102–103. *The sense of a place is often best conveyed by scenes that are typical and easily found, like this mountain lake, which shines in the glow of sunset light, capturing the beauty of the Colorado countryside.*

LEFT. *Three telling aspects of the Death Valley landscape are telescoped in this monochromatic composition: the distant Panamint Mountains, the salt flats in the valley, and the meandering road.*

OPPOSITE. *On the coast in Maine the red light of dawn briefly dramatizes the rocky landscape of Acadia National Park.*

place's distinctiveness. What is it about Yosemite Valley that takes our breath away? Is it the vastness of space? The shapes of the glaciated monoliths? The thin sprays of waterfalls surrounded by dense vegetation? What is it about the Tuscany countryside that seems so timeless and tranquil? Is it the gently rolling stony hills? The craggy villas and farmhouses framed by cypress trees? The intricate patchwork of ancient vineyards bathed in an ethereal light?

As we learn to identify the specific elements that contribute to a landscape's overall effect, we will succeed in capturing the essence of each place. This means understanding aspects of the terrain and its typical geological and botanical features. It means considering the quality of light that is unique to each place. It means organizing the elements of a vast space to create scale and graphic interest. And it means experimenting with a variety of lenses and perspectives.

Panoramas and Scenics

By definition panoramas and scenics encompass broad vistas. Therein lies a common problem in photographing landscapes: unless each image calls attention to something special, we may wind up with a series of nearly identical photographs. And instead of thrilling us, these photos will bore us with their sameness.

One way to avoid this pitfall is to experiment with different lenses, or a zoom lens, to vary perspectives. Wide-angle lenses from 24mm to 35mm are especially suited for a sweeping landscape. In addition, their great depth of field offers the advantage of featuring a subject in the foreground against an expansive background, with both in sharp focus. To maximize depth of field, focus on a point about one-third of the distance into the frame, slightly beyond the foreground subject, and close the lens down to f/16.

Telephoto lenses offer other possibilities, enabling you to isolate an important spot within a landscape, even at some distance. Their ability to "compress" space into a flat plane makes it possible to juxtapose two points within a landscape that may actually be quite far apart. For example, a nearby hillside

can appear to be just in front of mountains that are really in the far distance.

To create a sense of the third dimension, draw the viewer's eye into the photograph by incorporating converging lines, like those made by a road or train tracks.

Shooting a landscape requires a careful consideration of its light. Not only does an open vista generate reflections from land and vegetation, it also includes a scattering of light from the atmosphere. Such extraneous light can be controlled with filters. The polarizing filter may eliminate unwanted reflections and glare and deepen the blue of the sky. An ultraviolet (UV) filter cuts haze and increases clarity in high mountain regions. An 81A warming filter or Heliopan KR 1.5 red filter helps counteract the bluish tinge of midday and mountain light.

Remember to pay attention to the sky, including only as much as is needed to add interest and impact to your composition. Make sure that the horizon has integrity as a straight line. If the sky is part of your image, consider its shape within the frame. And camouflage a dull gray sky with tree foliage or tilt your camera down to eliminate it completely.

OPPOSITE. *To create evocative panoramas of quiet vistas, like this one of England's lake district, play up the soft colors and misty atmosphere.*

TOP. *A telephoto lens juxtaposes a field of desert wildflowers in Israel with the barren mountains of Moab in the distance.*

RIGHT. *A wide-angle lens encompasses a Maine pond, in the foreground, with rolling hills in the background.*

Earth Forms

There is a mysterious link between love and knowledge. Ideally, the more we know about someone or something, the stronger our love will be. This is also true of photography and nature. Those who love and photograph the natural world wish to understand it more completely. Our increased knowledge benefits our photographs, transforming them from mere responses to visual stimuli to reflections of enlightened interactions.

Our landscape photographs become more dramatic and evocative as we gain an understanding of the land. We become alert to beguiling forms and shapes, we learn to recognize distinctive features of the terrain, and we know where to find the hallmarks of each region. We can identify the age of mountains we visit. The jagged sort we find in the Rockies, the Alps, and the Himalayas indicate that they are young upstarts. The gently glaciated hills found in the northeastern Appalachians and in Maine's Acadia National Park are older.

Land forms wear the scars of time with grace and beauty, and we try to photograph these subjects as portraits, with respect for their many years. Glaciers have scoured mountain valleys into the characteristic U-shapes found in Yosemite National Park, while rivers have carved the earth's surface into V-shaped valleys, such as those in the Grand Canyon.

Other forces of erosion—wind, sand, and rain—have sculpted the earth into intriguing architectural, representational, and abstract forms. Their familiar shapes dot the landscape: flat-topped mesas and buttes, arches, windows, bridges, mushrooms, and spires all stand as revealing—but slowly changing—forms in erosion's inevitable path.

The story of the earth is embedded in the textures and colors of every rock face, and the very formation of the land is often visible. The whimsical swirls and layers found in sedimentary rock may be viewed as nature's own abstract paintings. Scouting with our eyes and cameras, we can truly find monumental images among them.

OPPOSITE. *A side view of Delicate Arch, a rock formation that draws visitors to Arches National Park, Utah, accentuates its shape through the play of light and shadow at sunset.*

LEFT. *A climb into the Swiss Alps reveals geologic formations such as this clear blue tarn fed by a mountain brook.*

ABOVE. *A desert bloom, such as this one in Israel's Jordan Valley, is a miracle of nature. Here poppies and wild grasses blanket normally barren hillsides.*

RIGHT. *Deserts reveal the effects of weathering on the landscape. Slow erosion shaped these pinnacles, while the daily impact of wind produces the intricate sand ripples found in Monument Valley in the American Southwest.*

Deserts

Of all natural environments, deserts bare their secrets most readily. Undulating sand dunes in shades of gray, coral, and white are etched with squiggly ripple markings. Fantastic eroded formations stand silhouetted against a pristine sky. Such stark, unadorned boldness translates beautifully to film, especially when enriched by the glow of light at dawn or dusk.

If you need further inspiration, study some of the famous photographs of desert landscapes and try to reproduce them. You will learn how to look at this environment with greater appreciation, and you will see the effort it takes to bring back outstanding shots.

The desert rewards those who venture beyond the "scenic vista" pull-offs. And because conditions in the desert are relatively predictable, you can plan to be in the right place at the right time to take successful photographs. Early spring finds cacti, yuccas, and assorted spiny species in flower, together with fields of poppies, anemones, wildflowers, and other bright and exotic desert plants.

While the desert has an inhospitable reputation, it is quite easy to manage with the right precautions. Stay on walking trails and paths, unless you know the territory well, since desert landmarks can be very confusing. Although you will not feel that you are perspiring in the dry desert climate, always carry—and make use of—extra drinking water.

Keep your camera gear as clean as possible by covering it with plastic bags until you are ready to shoot. Clean your gear daily with a soft brush especially made for camera equipment. Film that you are not carrying should be stored in a cooler. These are good photographic habits to develop when you travel and take pictures in the natural world.

ABOVE. *Canyonlands National Monument in Utah is a stark desert landscape of mesas and buttes softened by pastel pinks and mauves. A telephoto lens compresses the space and underexposure concentrates colors.*

LEFT. *A lone camel stands in the harsh wilderness of the Sinai Desert, providing scale and visual contrast.*

Forests and Woodlands

To handle the difficult forest light in Muir Woods, near San Francisco, California, the sun was positioned behind the silhouetted redwood trees.

A desert's stark terrain, well-defined forms, and brilliant light contrast sharply with a forest's lush vegetation, wealth of textures, and elusive light. And while a forest may be a more comfortable environment to visit, it is much more difficult to photograph.

It is almost impossible to capture on film the totality of the forest, simply because it is so hard to get enough distance from your subject. The best one can hope for is to find a clearing among the trees. Failing that, a wide-angle lens can push space back somewhat. Or try lying on the ground and shooting upward.

Working successfully with light is another problem in the woods. The dappled, high-contrast light that is so appealing to the eye is a disaster on film, placing spots on everything in sight. A polarizing filter helps unify the light somewhat. But even if you are photographing in what appears to be full shade, areas of bright light can produce "hot spots," which will catch the viewer's eye and detract from everything else in the photograph.

Forests and woodlands photograph best in low-contrast light, such as on a cloudy day, in mist, or very early in the morning. If the woods are very dark, overexpose slightly and use a warming filter. This filter may also be used if too much green light suffuses the atmosphere.

Take advantage of all the woodland textures by shooting vignettes and close-ups of ferns, mosses, lichens, mushrooms, leaves, and other vegetation, emphasizing color, clarity, and sharpness. Create interesting compositions by showing patterns in bark and repetition in tree trunks. Play to the strengths of the woodland environment for consistently good images.

ABOVE. *A black-and-white effect high-lights a few well-lit birches on the edge of a dark, snowy woods at the Donald M. Kendall Sculpture Garden in Purchase, New York.*

LEFT. *A stand of cedars outside Kyoto, Japan, form a composition based on line and color.*

To tame the bright light in this Coney Island seascape, the vivid sailboats were prominently placed in the composition and the dark portion of sky was metered and underexposed one stop.

SEASCAPES

The lure of the sea is so powerful that it has beckoned and inspired poets and painters through the centuries. And on its waves travelers have been carried to far-off places and have sought it as a refuge in its own right. The mesmerizing effect of the sea is such that photographers often neglect their cameras altogether. After all, it is relaxing just to sit back and focus our eyes on the endless horizon. And some of us may assume that the sea is the same the world over and thus, who could identify its location in a photograph?

While such turns of mind may be understandable, we will return with the greatest bounty if we heed the call of the sea, rouse ourselves, and really look at its visual riches. For the sea stirs our feelings as it reveals to us the interplay of sun, wind, and water. The most basic relationships of these natural elements become visible as we observe the meeting of water and sky or the confluence of land and sea. With no obstructions, we peer into infinite distance, sensing both the tranquility and tension of the scene.

This is the place of origins, where life itself began. This is a place of myths, where mysteries and ambiguities flourish. There is nothing definite or clear. There is only the timeless moment. Light changes by the instant, an early mist gives way to a merciless sun, or an enveloping fog lifts to reveal hovering clouds. Waves come and go, first crashing and spraying, then gently lapping the shore. A calm, glassy surface in the morning whips into a churning cauldron in the afternoon. It is always the same, and it is never the same. These are the images that call us to photograph seascapes: the desire to catch the evanescence and flux, the soothing buoyancy as well as the fearsome unknown.

Cruises

On cruises a photographer is free to concentrate on picture-taking. While on board there are few responsibilities and ample time to wander the decks in search of the best photo opportunities.

Sunrises and sunsets are excellent times to try for some dramatic shots or mood images, especially if clouds catch the colors of the sun. For the best exposure, meter the sea or the darker clouds rather than the sun. Look for special lighting effects, such as a beam of light on the water's surface or the "presence-of-God" rays of light emerging through clouds. Experiment with vertical as well as horizontal formats to avoid monotony.

Photograph each port of call as you approach and depart. Start shooting before you dock to get a progression of pictures, similar to our "snap-and-shift" procedure on land. Then observe the shore, looking for interesting locations and activities. If vendors surround you, consider them as potential subjects. If what they are selling is photogenic but not worth buying, take a photograph as a souvenir.

For photographers a disadvantage of a cruise is that you may be part of a crowd. If you care to do some serious photography, be prepared to venture away from the group, at least for a short time, to explore the place on your own.

Otherwise use the opportunity to take better pictures of your travel companions. Either on board or at a stop, they are sure to be enjoying themselves. Why not capture the good times on film? The sea itself makes a wonderful backdrop for such mementos. Just be sure to meter your companion's face if the surroundings are very bright.

A view of the Aegean Sea from a hilltop on Mykonos features an island church set against the rosy light of sunset.

To preserve memories of a sea voyage, include your cruise ship in travel photographs, as in this beachfront shot taken on one of Indonesia's tiny islands.

Capture the exuberance of a cruise by showing your travel companions having fun (but remember to meter people's faces to avoid silhouettes). Here passengers of Cunard's Sea Goddess enjoy the cool waters of a Malaysian beach as members of the crew serve champagne.

ABOVE. *In this image the gently curved shoreline on Mykonos successfully combines the coastal elements of water, sky, and land. Bright green algae add color and a slow shutter speed of 1/2 second blurs the moving water.*

OPPOSITE TOP. *An irregular design formed by foam at the edge of a slow-moving wave on Sand Beach in Maine provides an interesting counterpoint to the muted colors and simple horizontal lines in this beachfront composition.*

OPPOSITE BOTTOM. *A wide-angle overview of California's craggy coastline at Point Lobos sharpens the contrast of the succulent plants with the churning sea behind, just as it strikes the rocky shore.*

Beaches and Coastlines

The points where land, sea, and sky converge offer wonderful photographic possibilities. However, the most evocative images feature only one of these three elements in the starring role. The most important component should fill the largest portion of the frame.

If the land is dominant, accentuate its most interesting aspects: the stones or boulders along the shore, the jagged cliffs dropping to the sea, the fine white sand on the beach. The line between land and sea should draw the eye into the distance, and should be strong in its own right. The sense of the third dimension can be enhanced with a prominent foreground object, something a wide-angle lens helps achieve.

Water deserves the spotlight when it is very colorful or shows interesting motion. Bring out the brilliant blues and greens of the sea with your polarizing filter and, if necessary, underexpose slightly. Ektachrome and Fujichrome produce more dazzling blues and greens than other film.

Stop the motion of spray as it crashes on a rocky shore with a very fast shutter speed—1/250 of a second or faster—and time the release of the shutter to coincide exactly with the optimum moment. Watch a few repetitions before you take your shot, and use a telephoto lens to stay out of harm's way.

The sky may be the main event if the atmospheric light is especially alluring, or if the clouds and sun create a gorgeous display.

Whether land, sea, or sky plays the lead, good exposure requires special care at the shore. In the uniform light of misty or cloudy days, meter the land, not the sea or sky. Then shoot at the meter reading and overexpose slightly to avoid a dull look. In bright, high-contrast light, meter the highlights on rocks or trees so they will not turn white from overexposure. If the scene has too much reflected light from water and sand, use a polarizing filter or move to a position that will reduce glare. For sunset shots, meter the colorful clouds or sky away from the sun.

Waterfronts

Waterfronts are often hubs of human activity with lively businesses ranging from fishing boats and shipyards to pleasure boats and restaurants. Instead of the peace and tranquility one expects at the shoreline, there is a feeling of perpetual motion. Even a seemingly still scene vibrates with excitement. There is a cacophony of color in the houses. Reflections bounce and jostle one another. Birds take off and land nervously, as if they were trying to outdo one another.

Here is a setting that tests the photographer's eye for composition. Limiting the scope of each photograph to a relatively simply statement is the surest way to bring order to the waterfront chaos. Too much of anything will ruin the effect. Avoid overviews and discover vignettes and details. Take advantage of repeating shapes in boats, sails, pilings, and fishing paraphernalia.

And leave time for shots of people, many of them crusty characters who delight in showing off their latest catch or the boat they have owned for decades. Try to shoot them engaged in their work—repairing nets, drying fish, painting boats—for an added bit of local color.

OPPOSITE. *Reflections photographed from a bridge spanning a Dutch canal show the waterfront during an unusual moment of inactivity.*

TOP. *An azure sky and an array of boats in a marina in Cassis, France, convey the essence of a Mediterranean waterfront scene at sunrise.*

RIGHT. *Details of seafaring gear make colorful waterfront photographs. Lobster traps and buoys are typically found on a dock in Bass Harbor, Maine.*

CITYSCAPES

The idea of photographing cities is as old as photography itself. Since the camera's invention, photographers have captured the spirit of the metropolis, in all its luster and squalor, starting with the French inventor Louis-Jacques-Mandé Daguerre and his scenes of Paris, on through the harrowing images that Civil War photographer Mathew Brady took of Atlanta, to the evocative renditions of Alfred Stieglitz's New York and Josef Sudek's Prague.

To their advantage most of these photographs were intimately connected with the cities they portrayed. For traveling photographers, the trick is to get to know many aspects of an unfamiliar city as quickly as possible. Again, we fervently believe that the camera helps in the search for authentic, intense responses to new places, for the simple reason that photography forces us to look with more concentration and purpose.

City images tend to take on a formal look. The preponderance of architectural structures—skyscrapers, rectilinear buildings, bridges, streets—naturally turns our eye toward the arrangement of lines and geometric shapes. Become more conscious of the city environment in these formal ways, and make those lines and shapes work for you as graphic elements that add vitality to each image.

The variations in height within a city make it possible to try a variety of perspectives. Experiment with views that look up from street level; down from a cathedral, skyscraper, or hill; across a bridge; and through archways, gates, and windows. Also, remember to vary the distance from which you shoot to include overviews, vignettes, and details.

Finally, soften the hard edges of the city by incorporating curved lines, early morning mist, the light of street lamps, and people. Take a break from sightseeing and refresh yourself by finding elements typical of each city. These glimpses of the living world will give you greater insight and delight than any exhibition or lecture.

OPPOSITE. *A city's character is revealed in scenes of typical activities. Outdoor cafés, commonplace in Venice, allow individuals time to relax, absorb some sun, and enjoy views of the canal.*

ABOVE. *To convey the beauty of Paris, this sunset shot of the graceful bridges on the Seine was enhanced with a warming filter and by a slight underexposure.*

Skylines and Overviews

If only for the sake of photographing an "establishing shot," it is worthwhile to take a few overviews of each city you visit. Besides providing you with a photograph worthy of a postcard, an overview gives you a valuable orientation.

There are two natural perspectives for city overviews: from above and from a distance. You can climb or ride to the top of many tall buildings, towers, cathedrals, or the like for an overhead vantage point. Or cross a bridge, part of the way or to the other side of a river for an unobstructed viewpoint. Then look around and determine the location of the landmarks, those recognizable, identifying structures that are a "must" in your photographs.

When you are ready to start photographing, keep the following points in mind:

1. Do not show too much sky, unless it adds drama, color, or balance to your image.
2. Add graphic interest to your composition by using streets and roads as lines to lead the viewer's eye in a direction of your choice.
3. Use your telephoto lens to home in on portions of the overall scene.
4. Remember that the glow of sunrise or sunset can transform an ordinary overview into a scene of special beauty.
5. Pay attention to shadows and use them imaginatively. Also, polarize to cut through haze or to reduce reflections from walls and the windows of buildings.
6. At dusk combine natural light and artificial light from traffic, streetlamps, store windows, and floodlit structures to create surreal colors that the eye alone cannot see.

OPPOSITE. *Following a summer storm over Central Park a panoramic overview of New York City unites a brilliant skyline with a magnificent cloud formation.*

RIGHT. *This wide-angle overview of Florence shows the nearby roof of the Duomo, the city below, and the Tuscan hills in the distance.*

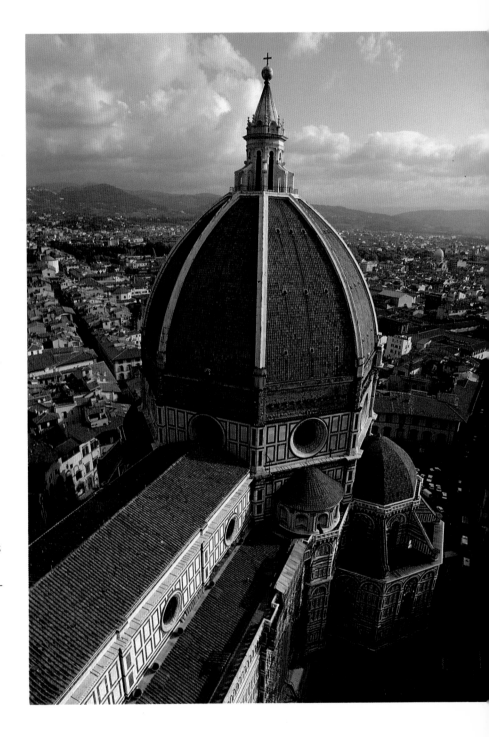

Street Scenes

Unlike overviews, which establish where you are, street scenes describe the mood of a city. These are the evocative shots that depend on your own appreciation of ordinary activities and commonplace sights.

The emphasis should be on the city's typical features. Observe the typical building materials and show them. Are the houses made of stone or painted adobe? Are the roofs thatched, tiled, or leaded? Are the streets cobbled, or are there canals? Are there unusual forms of transportation—double-decked buses, donkeys, trams, and so forth? These are all readily available subjects but often neglected, because they seem so usual. In fact, these details are what convey a sense of each place.

With each frame, remember to compose carefully. Use the lines of the sidewalk, the canal, or the bridge to make a visual point, as well as an editorial one. Always look at the scene as an arrangement of shapes, not just an assortment of things.

And do some exploring at different times of the day to show the effects of light and to capture various activities. Early morning is wonderful if you want empty streets and plazas, the hallmark of photographer Eugène Atget's work in Paris. A tranquil or eerie mood is fostered by the misty light just after sunrise. The wide-angle lens helps extend the space of open piazzas or narrow lanes.

At midday people and traffic add to the intensity of a city. Use your telephoto lens to compress and heighten the sense of crowdedness or to isolate bits and pieces from the whole. And after dark include the soft light of streetlamps, shop windows, and intimate dining scenes, creating weird color combinations with artificial light.

OPPOSITE. *The effect of mixed light sources—fluorescent light, tungsten light, and twilight—on daylight film transforms this ordinary street in Cassis into an otherworldly stage-set.*

ABOVE. *A group of people waiting for a bus on a street in Dakar, Senegal, form a colorful tableau within a rectilinear composition.*

Commerce

Commerce in Iquitos, Peru, is characterized by the unloading of produce from boats and its transport to the market for sale. This day's haul consisted of bananas from plantations upriver on the Amazon.

A city's raison d'être is commerce, as its economic activities establish it and maintain it. While many travelers take advantage of the opportunity to shop, few think of documenting this most basic part of city life with their cameras. This is a shame because some of the best bargains are the endless possibilities for images in markets.

Depending on the city, you will discover a wide range of shops, from elegant boutiques to street vendors, sometimes next to each other. Window displays can be quite telling of what is considered fashionable, often with unintended humor or irony. In less developed countries, open markets are a revelation in the art of orderly arrangements, with everything from produce to nuts and bolts in neat rows or piles. Wherever we travel, we find that local produce and handicrafts are interesting photographic subjects as well as colorful reminders of our excursions.

While scouting the markets, consider recording the local commercial practices and customs. In many countries, bargaining is done in earnest, with gestures and expressions as part of the ritual. The interaction between buyers and sellers is fun to photograph—whether the shoppers are natives or your travel companions. Even customary pinching or tasting of fruits is worth a shot.

And there is often a chance to watch artisans at work, creating the objects they will sell. Even if you are not planning to buy anything, you can still bring home a souvenir of the craft with your pictures.

Finally, signs usually animate commercial areas, from huge billboards and neon extravaganzas to simple homemade advertisements announcing what is available.

Commerce often takes place wherever a stand can be set up quickly. This
Istanbul vendor sells freshly caught fish from a pier on the Bosporus. The
simple composition uses horizontal lines and a monochromatic grey color
broken only by bright red tabletops and the fan-shaped display of fish.

Outdoor Dining

One of the great pleasures of travel, as well as one of its risks, is eating the local fare. Every city has a range of eateries, from the posh five-star, once-in-a-lifetime restaurants to the casual outdoor cafés, mom-and-pop bistros, and convenient but inelegant greasy spoons.

Because eating is part necessity, part adventure, and part ritual, it also offers wonderful opportunities for the traveling photographer. Furthermore, stopping for refreshment provides a welcome pause in the pace of traveling, allowing us time to contemplate our surroundings in an unhurried way. In countries where leisurely eating is the norm, your picture-taking is certain to allow you to enjoy this spirit by slowing you down a bit.

The ambiance of an eatery may be picturesque and photogenic even if it is less than ideal from the perspective of decor or hygiene. Think in terms of light, form, and color to create an interesting composition and to record a trip's worthwhile moment. Whether indoors or outdoors, a wide-angle lens helps to encompass foreground subjects, such as travel companions at a table, with the background scene.

Look at the people around you. There is usually a selection of local characters to choose from, including waiters, waitresses, cooks, and other customers. Take a few moments to observe their expressions and gestures, then try to capture some of their revealing movements. You will treasure these photos as rare and personal impressions of the local population.

TOP. *A wide-angle lens combines an open-air restaurant with Venice's Grand Canal and the buildings beyond. During a slow period, a willing waiter contributes to the atmosphere.*

LEFT. *Relaxing in an outdoor café is a favorite pastime in Aix-en-Provence and elsewhere in Europe.*

OPPOSITE. *The tablecloths echo the red of a nearby umbrella to spark this image of a Japanese teahouse in Takayama. Care was taken to compose the architecture as well as the reflections into a harmonious whole.*

Remember to include your traveling companions in these photographs. They are usually relaxed, having a drink, and enjoying a respite from sightseeing. Take a moment to catch their sense of ease as they wait for their meal to arrive.

And, when you are ready to sit down yourself, feast your eyes on the passing scene before you. Outdoor cafés are the perfect spot for people-watching. Sit, relax, observe, and within a few moments something interesting will come your way. Have your camera set for the light conditions of the day and for the focal distance you are likely to use. When you see that marvelous sight approaching, all you have to do is lift your camera and shoot.

Parks and Gardens

ABOVE. *The ornate Baroque gardens of the Villa Garzoni are shown against the simple setting of a Tuscany village. An overcast day tends to reduce the number of visitors and enriches the colors of the foliage.*

OPPOSITE. *A traveler may locate uncommon scenes, like this one in Japan, outside the major cities. The vermilion railing of Takayama's bridge, and the cherry trees and willows growing along the riverbank below, is a scene that may only be found by going off the beaten path.*

Parks and gardens are a city's oases, the places ordinary folks go to refresh their spirits. As a traveler, you should also visit public outdoor areas to gain insight into the character of the local population. Sit on a bench and watch a parade of people go by. You are likely to observe the national pastime, be it cricket, soccer, jogging, reading, sunning, smooching, or taking a nap. You will see families at play and can watch their interactions. You will also have a chance to take pictures in a relaxed manner.

As you explore the park or garden, notice the flora as well as the fauna. Each country has native plants that play a role in local garden designs. Beyond the most available flowers, however, each country also seems to prefer doing things in a distinct way. French and Italian parks and gardens may be quite formal, with trees planted in neat rows, and shrubs trimmed and shaped. English parks and gardens tend to have a more naturalistic look, with curved paths and flowing arrangements of flowers and grasses, as well as more formal components, such as topiary and hedge mazes. Japanese gardens attempt to perfect the look of nature, carefully placing and training plants so they create a harmonious, seemingly spontaneous whole. These variations reflect historic influences and national character, and when photographed, become vivid reminders of what you noticed and learned about both.

Parks and gardens also contain statuary and monuments that may be of artistic or historic importance. These may be made interesting by framing them with nearby greenery and by shooting them in beautiful early or late light.

The open spaces of parks and gardens often offer ideal vantage points from which to photograph the city skyline or nearby architecture. With wide-angle lenses, create a panoramic view, combining the park or garden with the skyline beyond. If a hotel or observation deck borders the park, try for an overview that incorporates the park and the surrounding cityscape.

OFF THE BEATEN PATH

Landscapes, seascapes, and cityscapes are the tried and true in travel photography. They picture the scenes that most travelers see, whether they are drawn to nature, the shore, or the centers of art and commerce. Fewer travelers venture off the beaten path to the outlying areas of a country, where traditions are enduring, where the rhythms of life are timeless, and where folk customs remain strong and visible.

Our world is becoming so homogenized that it is harder to tell one place from another. Even remote places have been overrun by development. It takes a bit of extra effort to seek out places where we can witness the unique qualities that attract passionate travelers in the first place. Once found, however, they reward us richly. The search may have a personal purpose, such as returning to a village of family origin. Or it may be to pursue an ongoing interest, something teachers often do when they visit places of literary or historic importance.

Or it may be pure chance. Some years ago on a trip to Switzerland to research high-tech dams, we stopped for a few days in the village of Evolene, in the mountains overlooking the Rhône Valley. The region was crisscrossed by old cattle paths now also used by hikers. We decided to walk these narrow trails for exercise and fresh air.

Within a few minute of leaving Evolene, we saw a field with women in traditional dirndls cutting hay with the slow, graceful sweep of long scythes. Down another path, we came across a preserved village of houses built on stone pilings. We noticed a patio set with wooden tables and benches, where a man at a wood grill was preparing raclette, the region's peasant dish, made from various cheeses, melted and scraped onto a wooden plate and served with small red potatoes.

Within a few moments we had given up our original plan to eat at our hotel. Instead we joined a group of knowledgeable visitors from around the world who had made a pilgrimage to this very patio just for this experience. We were lucky to be in the right place at the right time, but it never would have happened if we had stayed on the main roads or stuck to a rigid travel schedule. You may be surprised and delighted to find that places off the beaten path—the small villages and the countryside—are both hospitable and eminently photogenic.

Villages

The village of Sloten, Holland, is actually quaint and neat, and its residents are friendly. But the gnarled trees that line the streets give it a decidedly spooky appearance. A 16mm wide-angle rectilinear fisheye lens exaggerates the weird shapes of the trees.

In countries around the world the most consistently intriguing places we have visited are villages. This is partly because village life is so different from our very "modern" everyday existence, and partly because we have found the people and sights so dependably enchanting and surprising. This has been especially true in less developed countries, where the local people's curiosity about us has overcome whatever fears and suspicions they may have had. In more developed countries, the villages themselves have held our interest for their traditional architecture and lifestyle. In our travels in West Africa, India, Papua New Guinea, and Southeast Asia, the rhythms of daily life were more visible, and the people more willing to include us in their affairs. Whatever fears we may have had beforehand about going into unfamiliar territory were always quickly dispelled by the uniformly warm reception we received.

One memorable encounter with friendly villagers occurred during a journey we made to an oracle in northern Ghana. We hiked past several villages in a valley before climbing to the hills where the oracle was located. Along the way, we came upon a large compound housing an extended family. We were escorted to the village chief, who welcomed us, offered us one of his villagers as a guide, and, on our return, presented us with a goat as a sign of good will between us.

In a sense, visiting villages gives the earnest, respectful traveler a chance to learn about anthropology. The rituals of village life are often celebrated in indigenous festivals that resonate powerfully in the souls of the population. Timing a visit to coincide with a festival is certain to be rewarding.

Village housing is often a study in ingenuity, myth, and artistic expression. In West Africa, village women paint intricate geometric designs on the outer walls of their compounds. The structures in Tarajaland, Indonesia, are shaped like spaceships in the belief that the people came from another planet and will return there after death.

And the people themselves retain customs of dress, movement, and gesture that recall another time, when cultural differences were more pronounced. This vanishing world of traditional life should be witnessed, if possible, in person—and with a camera.

Countryside

In landscape photographs many travelers are only interested in capturing the grandeur of the wilderness. Pastoral scenes receive far less attention, even though they are often equally rewarding. Part of the reason may be that successful pictures of the countryside rely more on the visual imagination of the photographer. Instead of majestic peaks and valleys, there are gently rolling hills, sometimes carved with ancient terraces, and flat expanses that may stretch to infinity. How does one transform such undramatic terrain into the stuff of magnificent photographs?

Here are some answers:

1. Think of the contours of the land as assets, not liabilities. Use the natural curves and horizontal lines as graphic elements in your compositions.
2. Emphasize the colors and textures of the land. The exact color of green will depend on the crop that is growing. Other colors emerge with a change of crop or season. Holland's spring bulbs blanket the countryside with their brilliant colors, while autumn brings out the gold of a wheat field or the russet of a vineyard. Each crop's texture can be a source of photographic enrichment, both in scenics, which show the patchwork of fields, and in vignettes, which bring textural features into high relief.
3. Use the land as a counterpoint for other features, such as farmhouses, barns, haystacks, and an expanse of sky. In the low, warm light at the extremes of the day, sidelight creates deep shadows that set off any structures on the land, bringing out the texture of barn siding or hay in a most dramatic way. And the vast, open sky can be used as a block of pure blue balancing the land below, or as a point of interest in its own right, awash with clouds of

Wandering into Japan's countryside can be a welcome change of pace from its frenetic cities. Such open spaces as this hillside covered with wild azaleas are a visual treasure for visitors to nearby Kyoto.

every shape and kind. Try a polarizing filter to add contrast between the clouds and a blue sky.
4. Take advantage of the way weather changes the countryside. From early morning mist, to rolling thunderclouds, to dazzling sunshine, this is where the light hits the landscape most visibly, providing the alert traveler with many chances to make the photographs that will convey a personal sense of place.

6
Real People

"The street is a theatre where characters of every social class and circumstance, every age, and every physical type appear. To the imaginative eye, it is a theater where mundane events are transformed into metaphors."

SUSAN KISMERIC, 1990

TRAVELING COMPANIONS

On a trip the people we are most likely to portray are our travel companions. Unfortunately, instead of creating natural, personal images of family and friends, many photographers do not vary the way people are posed and show them standing exactly the same way in front of such famous sites as the Eiffel Tower or the Taj Mahal. Since travel companions in these pictures are often portrayed at a distance, their faces are barely recognizable. Expecting to include in a photograph both your companions and the sight—and hoping to do so successfully—is sometimes unrealistic.

Our general advice for those who want better photographs of their travel companions is to avoid the most common mistakes. First of all, do not automatically require your family and friends to pose. Oddly enough this method works well for people you do not know, and we will discuss this point later on. Since you know your family and friends, and understand their expressions and moods, you can anticipate their reactions. Make the most of this knowledge and take candid pictures of them whenever possible. We will discuss how best to create these kinds of photographs in the next few pages.

Also, move in closer so your companions' faces become the dominant features of a picture. The viewer's eye should gravitate toward the face first and only later on take in the rest of the scene.

Do not be afraid to play the role of director. Engage the cooperation of your subjects, especially in repeating a

PAGES 136–137. *Look for people performing daily tasks, like these Ghanaian fishermen pulling in the day's catch with a huge net. Their muted reflections on the watery shore underscore their exertion and enhance the image.*

momentary action. If you need their help, ask for it. Your photograph may not be totally spontaneous, but it is likely to be livelier than the standard sort. Or, you may wish to involve yourself to a greater degree by explaining to your companions the kind of picture you envision. They will quickly get into the spirit of your efforts, assisting you by performing on cue with the actions and interactions you requested.

These first suggestions will help you avoid the usual posed photographs. Further steps, described on the next few pages, will advance you to the point of capturing the most memorable moments of a travel experience with those closest to you.

ABOVE. *Our colorfully clad travel companions add a bright note to this misty scene of a dinghy float on Alaska's Mendenhall River. A fast shutter speed stops the boat's motion.*

LEFT. *It is often effective to photograph companions taking pictures. This couple on a honeymoon cruise in Indonesia took every opportunity to record each other's activities. A polarizing filter removes glare to enrich the water's turquoise color.*

OPPOSITE. *During a desert trip in Jordan an important memory was the moment two thirsty companions dropped to the ground to lap up water from a stream.*

Souvenirs

Recording a child's joy at greeting a Disney character is a coveted souvenir for many traveling photographers. Improve the odds of success by allowing the child a moment to savor the experience. Then attract the youngster's attention, as in this shot taken at Disneyworld in Florida. Fill-in flash removes unwanted shadows and unifies the light.

Traveling with companions inevitably confronts us with moments that demand to be preserved but which we frequently overlook. Among these are times of emotional intensity. We call these kinds of photographs souvenirs, because they serve as treasured reminders of special travel memories we want to relive for years to come. Our feelings may be stirred by our reactions to a shared experience or to an evocative setting.

Think of the exhilaration of climbing to the peak of a mountain and recording our friends with their victorious smiles and proud hand clasps. Or imagine portraying the fascination and delight of children at a puppet show or a circus. Or remember how it was to watch the sun setting over the mountains and to capture the beauty and tranquility of the scene with our companions in the photo.

What makes such travel pictures rare is our involvement in the moment. It is extremely difficult to be absorbed in the immediate experience and still be able to distance ourselves to observe our companions and decide to photograph them.

Undoubtedly, many such moments will go unrecorded because of this inherent difficulty. Nor should we become so aggressive in our pursuit of these photographs that we spoil the mood or generate resentment. But as we become increasingly sensitive to noteworthy travel situations, we will recognize such moments and make the effort to capture them on film in a respectful way.

Creating souvenirs involves an understanding of human nature and the ability to anticipate people's reactions. If you think in advance about your day's travel plans and the possible emotional reactions you might witness, you will be ready to go into action with your camera when the magical moment arrives. Add some shots to flesh out the story—close-ups of the puppets, pictures during the climb, and scenics of the surroundings—and your pictures will serve as a memorable narration.

A child's pleasure in feeding pigeons on Venice's Piazza San Marco is a souvenir to treasure. A wide-angle lens incorporates the special setting behind the featured person.

Snapshots

A different photographic approach is needed for capturing unrepeatable moments that cannot be fully anticipated. For example, travel companions may be talking animatedly with one another or laughing together, and you may want to preserve their spontaneous expressions or gestures.

Such snapshots depend on the photographer's skill and quickness and demand vision, accuracy, and creativity. The photographer needs to recognize a revealing situation, have a camera ready, speedily frame the shot, and shoot. This is an ideal time to rely on automatic settings for exposure and focus, if your camera has them. The important thing is not to hesitate. Forget about being a perfectionist. Time lost in getting a better composition and focus may mean losing the picture altogether.

Of course, no such photographs are possible unless a camera is at hand. A small camera that fits into a purse or side pack is a great asset for taking snapshots, especially if companions are a short distance from you. (Photographing people at more than 15 feet [4.6 meters] may require more specialized equipment, as we discuss later in this chapter.)

As a general rule, set your shutter speed at 1/125 of a second or faster, especially if you are trying to portray facial expressions. Slower speeds will produce blurs where there is movement. Having the subject's hands blurred is not a problem, as long as the face is reasonably sharp. If the light is too low to use a fast shutter speed, activate your flash. The burst of light will freeze any motion.

It may turn out that the momentary situation continues, and you have time to work on the photograph with greater care. Under these circumstances, your companions can be "caught in the act," as the next section explains.

A snapshot recalls the fleeting instant when a monkey in a Gambian nature preserve became curious about a companion's camera. At a distance of five feet, a standard lens magnifies the subject.

Caught in the Act

Most traveling photographers are delighted to have photographs that show their companions engaged in activities during the trip. The possibilities are limited only by your interests and imagination: horseback riding, skiing, boating, shopping, and smelling flowers are just a few of the possibilities.

Unlike situations that require snapshots, these activities are usually predictable and repeatable. That is, the photographer can anticipate that certain actions are likely to occur. Your husband will climb into the saddle; your wife will spin on the dance floor; on the carousel your child will display delight; to reach the boat your friend will leap from the dock.

Prepared for these occurrences, the photographer can be ready to take a picture. In many instances, if the shot is missed when the action first occurs, it can be repeated for the camera. The child on the amusement ride, for example, will come into view again and again. A wife can be cajoled into recreating her exciting dance moves. But if the specific moment is lost forever, remember that another one is likely to occur soon enough. Do not let disappointment spoil your fun.

Catching people in the act requires stopping them in midmotion. Whenever possible, set your shutter speed at 1/125 of a second or faster, even if it means using a wide open aperture. Indoors, at night, or in low outdoor light conditions, when a fast shutter speed is impossible, use your flash to freeze the action. Fast films in the 400 to 1000 ISO range also help in stopping movement.

A toddler who could not contain her happiness during a puppet parade in Takayama, Japan, is caught in a delightfully compromising pose.

PORTRAYING STRANGERS

There is a great difference between photographing people you know and those you do not know. First, we cannot be sure how a stranger will feel about being photographed. Will the person cooperate or resist? Will the subject be flattered or offended? Taking pictures of strangers may even pose a danger to the photographer—either because of local taboos or laws.

Then, depending on the answers to these questions and the image we want to create, should we photograph openly and visibly, perhaps asking permission to pose our subject? Or should we shoot from a hidden vantage point, trying for the most candid effects?

In fact, most photographers prefer taking candid shots, without making their subjects aware of them, because they assume this produces a more spontaneous, natural image. However, an "invisible" photographer has to be fairly far away from a subject. As a result, the image of this very fascinating person will be disappointingly small, and often, there will be intrusive people and objects. The alternative is to use a powerful telephoto lens, which entails other compromises, photographically speaking.

Many people prefer to "shoot from the hip," because they feel that it spares them the discomfort of having to interact with a stranger. On the contrary, we can say without hesitation that a real advantage of making your intentions known is the necessity of establishing communication with your subject.

We believe that a policy of candor is not only practical but also ethical. On the practical side, we have always been amazed by the willingness of people to be photographed. At first they may be shy or curious about why we want to take their picture, but they have been good-natured and helpful.

They have even shown a willingness to move into better light, turn so there is a more effective backdrop, and make any number of other small adjustments to help us represent them in a better way.

On the ethical side, we feel that asking a stranger if we can take a photograph gives the subject control, through the right of refusal. If someone says, "No," and means it—not merely a polite refusal or shy reluctance—then we move on to someone else who does not mind. With few exceptions, others can be found to substitute without a loss to our photographic integrity. And the truth is that there are far fewer refusals than acceptances. Most subjects sense our respect for them by the very act of asking.

Of course, we try to lay the groundwork for the request first by developing an interaction: ask about or buy what a market vendor is selling; comment on a lovely baby; notice something, or ask a question. Even if we do not speak the native language, a smile and friendly demeanor will go a long way toward breaking the ice. Then a gesture toward the camera and an expression such as "okay?" is all that is needed.

There are times when we must be unobtrusive to get a particular photograph, and we will discuss those instances shortly. Most situations, however, will yield the photographic memento through a combination of sensitivity and daring. And the bonus for the photographer is a better sense of what the people of the area are like. Snatches of friendly conversation have often led to discoveries about commonalities we did not know existed and to invitations to homes and festivities that would never have occurred if all we had done was to shoot from the shadows of obscurity.

Strangers are often much more cooperative subjects than many traveling photographers imagine. This family in Papua, New Guinea, proudly posed for a group portrait, bedecked in ceremonial regalia.

Understanding Local Customs

It is especially important for travel photographers to develop a balance between sensitivity and daring. It also helps to understand which cultural boundaries to respect, and which hesitations are personal and can be overcome.

When we interact with people in unfamiliar societies, we may encounter a resistance to photography. There are cultures that hold deep suspicions about photography, even to the point of outlawing it. But these are so rare that this consideration should not worry most traveling photographers.

Local customs, superstitions, and taboos may explain why people may not want to be photographed. Photographers who have worked with members of cultures that oppose iconography—for example, Islamic women and Hasidic Jews—have found that even such rigid attitudes can be overcome by forming a positive relationship within the community. Building trust, however, takes more time than most traveling photographers can spare. So within these cultures, do not press too hard if your request to photograph is refused. Or resort to being unobtrusive in your picture-taking.

People in some less developed countries believe that the photographer is taking advantage of them and will benefit financially from the pictures taken. Often, these people are willing to work out a deal, and, if you offer money, the photograph can be yours. But do not automatically pay everyone who asks. We have found other subjects—just as interesting, and sometimes more so—willing to be photographed without remuneration.

But the most common reason for people's reluctance to be photographed is simple shyness and unfamiliarity. If we imagine being approached by a stranger who asks to photograph us, we can well understand that reaction. Often a little cajoling and coaxing, a little reassurance, an offer to allow that person to look through the camera will go a long way toward breaking down resistance. On the other hand, there are many places where people pose eagerly and actually ask to have their pictures taken.

Understanding human nature is just as important as being sensitive to cultural differences. Again, the photographer who establishes some connection with the subject before trying to take a picture will likely have greater cooperation and success. But regardless of how willing or unwilling the subject may be, the photographer will still need daring, determination, and persistence to go after an image.

A bride smiled shyly when she saw us photographing her at the Heian Shrine in Kyoto. A 250mm lens was needed to fill the frame from a considerable distance of over 100 feet.

Working "on the Sly"

When faced with a situation that demands the photographer to work "on the sly," there are two slightly deceptive practices that have proven effective in getting the picture.

An unobtrusive option entails using a moderate telephoto lens in the 100mm range. This lens is invaluable if the photographer needs to be 20 to 30 feet (7m to 10m) away and is interested in capturing the people within their immediate environment. In markets, for example, it is possible to photograph merchants or local customers surrounded by their wares. The 100mm lens allows the photographer to remain unobtrusive at a comfortable distance from the subject, and yet the lens is not so powerful that camera shake or movement will cause major problems. This is also the lens of choice at a closer distance for portraits taken with the subject's awareness.

A bolder approach involves duping your photographic prey by using a wide-angle lens in the 28mm to 20mm range, which gets you close to the subject, while including much of the surrounding scene. This option works best if the photographer seems very intent on photographing the scene and aims the camera so it does not directly face the people. Because of the wide breadth of this lens, the people will be incorporated within the frame, without their knowledge or awareness. Even if challenged or questioned, the photographer can protest innocence and point in the direction of the apparent subject.

TOP. *Religious customs practiced in public places are fascinating to witness and photograph. In Varanasi, India, townspeople and pilgrims perform the daily ritual of morning ablutions in the Ganges River. A telephoto lens frames the scene from a hired boat, and high-speed film helps contend with problems of motion and low light.*

RIGHT. *With no one to ride his ponies in the middle of the day, this Parisian entrepreneur pays no attention to the photographer's attempts to portray him in a moment of relaxation.*

To Pose or Not To Pose

To pose or not to pose: this question comes up again and again for traveling photographers interested in taking pictures of strangers.

There is undoubtedly a loss of spontaneity when we ask someone to "perform" for the camera. We would all prefer to capture the natural expressions, gestures, and actions of our subjects just as they are occurring. Realistically, we would have to devote enormous amounts of time and energy to get totally candid photographs. To start we would have to be in the right place at the right moment, and we would need enough light to be able to shoot at a shutter speed of faster than 1/60 of a second to avoid a blurred image.

We may sometimes get lucky and bring back such shots, and we surely treasure them when we do. But since a conflu-ence of ideal circumstances is rare, and since the traveling photographer is always faced with the pressure of time, it is expedient, and sometimes preferable, to pose our subjects. Posing, however, need not be an exercise in uninspired for-mality. It is possible to pose people in interesting and varied ways.

Here are a few suggestions:
1. Ask if you can photograph the subject in the process of an activity. Vendors, craftsmen, fishermen are often too busy to stop what they are doing, nor would you want them to. Let them do their work while you do yours.
2. Groups are natural targets for posing, and their freewheel-ing interactions often continue as you snap away. Friends,

Children of straw weavers in northern Ghana learn their parents' craft through play and example. Close to this young boy are a sleeping mat and broom made by his family. Meter both light and dark colors in such high-con-trast conditions; then choose an exposure setting in between.

families, and children in groups provide mutual support and a lively give and take, which the camera picks up readily.

3. Individuals pose more readily when they have the time to do so. Do not interfere with people's work or routines when they are at their busiest. Come back after rush hour, if your subject can be found in a specific location.

4. When you take the time to pose someone, make it worthwhile. Determine the best possible light, surroundings, and background on your subject before you set up the shot. Do not lose the opportunity to produce a truly beautiful image by rushing or feeling guilty about bothering the person. If your subject has agreed to be photographed, use that willingness to your advantage, but be respectful of your subject's time by planning first. As a gesture of appreciation, take the person's name and address, and remember to send a copy of the photograph you took.

The unexpected sight of an athletic young man bathing in a shallow river in Ghana meant working with speed to capture his image while he was unaware that he was being photographed.

Background Information

An important advantage of posing is the control we gain in placing a subject within the immediate setting. This advantage is lost, however, if we fail to exercise care. While our eye tends to isolate the person who interests us, the camera also records many things we may not notice, in front of a subject and, especially, in the background.

A subject's background serves as a framework, and paying attention to it is the first step toward creating the image we envision. As we become more aware of the background, we can decide which aspects of it to integrate into our composition.

There are two important points to consider about the background in relationship to the subject:

1. How sharp should the background be? If the background contributes to the image, keep it sharp, using the highest possible f-stop—at least f/8—to retain the maximum amount of detail. For example, a vendor in a market can be shown with the contents of his shop or a boatman can be portrayed against a city backdrop.

   On the other hand, if the background is unpleasant or irrelevant, it can be blurred out by opening up your aperture to its widest setting and moving the subject a few feet forward—toward you and away from the backdrop.

2. How much contrast is there between the subject and the background? Contrast refers to differences in the intensity of light or color between two elements in a photograph. High-contrast situations are those with areas of bright light and deep shadow, or with extreme color combinations. Low-contrast conditions have uniform light or colors of similar hue or intensity.

   A dark background is often desirable for portraits because the subject stands out clearly. Placing your subject against an area in shadow and exposing for the highlights or bright areas of the face will cause the background to

ABOVE. *The boxy shapes and startling colors of this Lower East Side tenement in New York City enliven the background behind this Latino man and his mother.*

OPPOSITE. *The city of Varanasi on India's Ganges River glows behind our rowing boatman. Composed with a moderate wide-angle lens so the boat and shoreline are parallel, the exposure favors the background, leaving the boatman's face in shadow.*

darken. People with very dark complexions are better set off against a less dark background.

When contrast can not be achieved through light differences, try finding a background with a single color. A simple background is most effective for featuring a person. Too many colors in the background, even if they are partially blurred out, will detract from your main point of interest.

THE DECISIVE MOMENT

By anticipating the action, the photographer was prepared for the instant when this Israeli couple went from joking and flirting to stealing a kiss.

The best photographs of people are those with a special spark, that is, an element of universality and recognition that allows the viewer to identify with the subject. One way to produce that quality is to trigger the shutter at the "decisive moment," a phrase coined by the influential French photographer Henri Cartier-Bresson.

The decisive moment refers to the instant when action is at its peak, at its most telling. A physical movement, such as a leap, may reach its decisive moment at its highest point. But if the photograph shows a child leaping into a puddle, the decisive moment may just as well be the instant of impact.

Facial expressions and gestures also have their decisive moments, whether captured in candid or posed photographs. There is an instant when the person's character shines through most truly, when real emotions show, or when a posture or hand movement typical of the individual or the culture is evident. These evanescent moments are the gems photographers mine.

While they are the most rewarding images, they are also the most demanding. Catching people at the decisive moment requires awareness and vigilance on the part of the photographer. The subject must be watched—virtually stalked—when the circumstances seem ripe, and the photographer must develop enough understanding of the subject's ways to anticipate the next move.

The more familiar the photographer is with the subject and the situation, the greater the likelihood of success. For there is a flow or rhythm to movements—whether in dance, sports, or ordinary human interactions—that an astute photographer will recognize.

In less familiar circumstances, it is worthwhile to take a little time to observe what is going on. Is the couple about to embrace or kiss? Is the child mirroring a parent's expression or gesture? Are the worshipers engaged in traditional religious rituals? Are vendors trying to convince customers to purchase their wares? Are the women gossiping or relaxing in characteristic fashion?

Whenever possible, notice patterns of human action, reaction, and interaction, before snapping the shutter. This is hard to do while moving around. The chance of seeing, and, therefore, photographing everyday events that enrich travel photographs is increased by staying in a promising spot and observing patiently. Invariably, a decisive moment will occur wherever people congregate.

A wait-and-watch approach also enables the photographer to compose in advance, to prepare to shoot at the right moment. Since timing is so vital, keep in mind that the shutter must be released just before the decisive moment occurs. Once the moment takes place, it is too late to record it. That is why the ability to anticipate is so important.

Of course, if an unexpected situation cries out for immortality, instinct and speed must take over. Well-honed skills and automatic camera features offer assistance, but there is no time to hesitate or to worry about perfect composition. This is the time to shoot first and hope for the best. If luck prevails, we will have caught a moment to remember.

A spot just outside a Japanese sweetshop was ideal for stalking happy customers like this boy enjoying a sticky ricecake at a decisive moment.

The Daily Round

One of the unfortunate limitations of travel is the lack of time to view, far less to savor, the way people live. That is why the experienced traveler, unlike the sightseer, searches for the ordinary. Similarly, the traveling photographer seeks scenes of personal discovery that characterize and signify everyday existence for the local population.

This is no simple feat, especially in western cultures, where business is generally conducted in private. But it may be achieved if we consider the obvious worth photographing. This notion struck us anew when we were in India. We noticed a construction site with scaffolding made of what looked like flimsy saplings tied with jute. The thin workmen climbed this makeshift contraption readily, and performed various duties. Naturally, we took photographs to show the disparity between cultures but also to marvel at the ingenuity of these laborers.

Only later did we wonder how many tourists of the millions who visit our city, New York, would think to take pictures of construction crews. Would not these pictures comment on activities in the ever-renewing metropolis? Would not the photos depict some of the quintessential characters of the city? The streets, residential areas, parks, beaches, shopping districts, and eateries of western cultures are rich with such possibilities.

In many cultures, however, ordinary people do everyday things right in the open. It becomes easy and fascinating to observe people engaged in an endless variety of activities in open markets, along streets and seashores, and in their own yards and doorways. Without disturbing their privacy, it is possible to view and portray people leading their daily lives and to gain insight into their lives.

ABOVE. *On Malta, living rooms extend onto sidewalks, with families greeting neighbors and watching the passing scene.*

OPPOSITE. *The rhythm of the daily round includes moments to slow down. To escape the afternoon heat in northern Ghana, children and elders gather beneath huge baobab trees.*

Markets and Bazaars

In European countries we make a habit of visiting a local outdoor food market early in the morning. This is when farmers set up stands in the town center to sell locally produced fruits, vegetables, cheeses, and meats. This tradition of fresh food is flourishing, despite the advent of supermarkets. When we finish shooting, we buy a delicious lunch to enjoy al fresco later in the day.

The markets of Africa, Asia, and South America can be huge open-air extravaganzas, often on specific days of the week. It is worthwhile to find out when markets are open, for they draw a colorful assortment of people and products. There are markets where domestic animals, such as camels or sheep, are sold and handicraft markets, where intricate basketry or locally made textiles are offered. And, of course, there are food markets everywhere.

Look for interesting faces among the vendors and customers, for attractive displays of goods, and for those momentary interactions that surface now and again. To capture the excitement of a marketplace, find a spot that has visual potential. Then frame your shot and stay alert. Something fascinating is sure to happen.

A zoom lens is a real boon in markets, especially one in the 28mm to 90mm range, which has wide-angle to moderate telephoto capacity. Use the wide-angle extreme for getting in close and combining the people with their surroundings. Rely on the telephoto extreme for shooting a bit further away and still getting facial details.

Fast film from 200 to 400 ISO helps in markets that are dimly lit, such as those under canopies or indoors. And use the automatic features of your camera for exposure and focusing so you can concentrate on looking and composing quickly.

OPPOSITE. *Markets like this one in Iquitos, Peru offer travelers examples of local color and character. To compose this "slice of life," the vendor was set among her round bowls of fruit juice.*

LEFT. *With knife in hand, this Sicilian fishmonger is about to cut into a large eel. The bright tungsten lights in his stall made the photo possible.*

BELOW. *Long packets of rice wrapped in dried leaves enliven this shot of a roadside stand on the Indonesian island of Sulawesi.*

People at Work

A good way to discover everyday activities to photograph in unfamiliar societies is by watching people at work, especially in countries where work is done outdoors or in accessible indoor areas.

Try beginning with craftspeople and artisans, for wherever one finds weavers, potters, wood- or stonecarvers, and painters, one is likely to find promising subjects to be photographed at decisive moments. Observe them for a while before you begin photographing. Notice the routines and rhythms of their work. Develop a feel for the timing of their movements. Then use a fast shutter speed to freeze the moment or experiment with a slow shutter speed to capture the motion in each stroke.

Butchers, bakers, tailors, waiters, greengrocers, fishermen, and fishmongers are often willing subjects, as long as you don't interfere with their business. A good way to enlist their cooperation is to buy something first. Again, observe the moments of greatest interest. Is it when a customer is paying? When business is brisk and the pace is harried? Or when there is a lull that allows expressions to return to normal?

People in the transportation field are also prime subjects: cabbies, train conductors, boatmen, and rickshaw drivers. Catch them while you are using their services, or just before, or after. In some places, there is an aggressive ritual by which drivers solicit riders. Try photographing the interaction when an offer is first made, or when the deal is finally struck.

Finally, there is everyday domestic work. In the countryside this may include farming or ranching chores. In small towns, there is washing and cleaning. These simple tasks, recorded on film, help recreate the tenor of the places we visit.

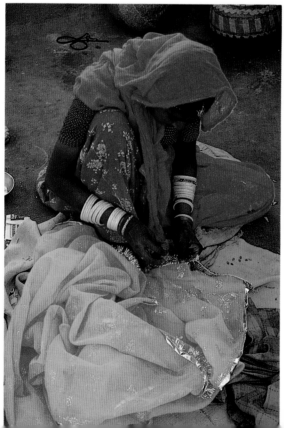

TOP. *Ghanaian men traditionally weave Kente cloth in narrow strips that are sewn together. Here a villager outside Kumasi works at his loom.*

LEFT. *A young Rajasthani woman sits on the ground while sewing glittery trim on a colorful sari that is the region's traditional fashion.*

People at Play

Travel offers the chance to photograph people at play after their work is done. Since leisure activities most often occur in the open, they may be photographed easily. And because people are relaxed and having fun, they are also more willing to be photographed.

Observe national pastimes and festivities. Depending on where you are traveling, these can be anything from a lively game of street soccer to an intense chess match on a park bench. And do not neglect people of all ages simply enjoying themselves, at parades, picnics, beaches, and even in their backyards.

Note that decisive moments may occur at the instant that the game is won or at other moments of tension and excitement. A photograph of a ball in midair or a well-placed kick can be just as desirable as a picture of the final goal being scored. Keep an eye on the players' and the observers' faces.

Their expressions may convey a spirit of enjoyment better than any other action.

Play can also be quiet and simple. Watch people strolling in the park, or chatting serenely on a bench, or absorbed in reading on a blanket. Even a subject who is napping can be interesting, given the right surroundings and expression.

Children at play are irresistible, even to strangers. The way a child's play mimics so much of the adult world is fascinating, as is the ingenuity of children who rely on their own creativity to devise playthings.

For fast-paced activities, shoot at a shutter speed of 1/125 of a second or faster. Also, try panning by following a runner or skater with the camera while in motion, but with a slow shutter speed of 1/8 to 1/30 of a second. A zoom telephoto lens is helpful for framing quickly and getting closer to the action.

Japanese schoolgirls in uniforms have fun hopping from stone to stone in the water garden of the Heian Shrine in Kyoto.

ABOVE. *Although hesitant and suspicious about being photographed, this woman in Jodhpur, India, agreed to move to a shaded spot for this portrait.*

OPPOSITE. *This woman's portrait—taken with fill-in flash and from a low angle to minimize nearby distractions—features a dramatic hat and other festive accessories worn in an Easter Parade in New York City.*

PORTRAITS

When we think of people, most often we think of faces. More than the things they do at work or play, more than their inter-actions, more than the distinctive clothing they wear or the cultural habits they exhibit, it is their faces that attract us.

What becomes apparent to the traveling photographer is the infinite variety of faces, each communicating an emotion or mood. The face may be a mask, hiding a person's feelings and circumstances. Or the face may be a conduit to the heart and soul, revealing inner doubts or strengths that could not be otherwise defined.

The very process of photographing strangers' faces breaks down barriers. We may begin with an attitude that emphasizes the differences between us: "Look at how odd these people are! See how exotic they look." As soon as we begin to photo-graph those faces, that attitude begins to change, because for any facial portrait we strive to win our subject's cooperation. We smile and converse. We ask some questions, work through our mutual confusion, and try to reassure our subject of our good intentions. We must maintain a relaxed, friendly atmos-phere while we fiddle with camera gear and figure out the best placement for our subject.

We have repeated this procedure, through many variations, in countries all over the world. Invariably, instead of being impatient and irritable—as we imagine ourselves becoming in similar circumstances—our subjects have displayed remarkable willingness, even eagerness, to be partners in our enterprise.

We once stopped at a village outside of Kumasi, the ancient central city of Ghana, seeing a fascinating man standing in a doorway. We approached him, asked about the name of the vil-lage and his position in it. In lilting West African English, he explained that he was the chief of the village. He agreed to let us take some pictures of him right there in the doorway.

After we completed our initial shooting, he invited us

inside, to meet his family and associates, and to arrange a proper "royal" portrait. The official stool, umbrella, and red crown were brought out, and a formal sitting took place. Our boldness increased, and we asked to reposition the entourage in front of a painted blue wall in the compound. There, the formal group shot was retaken and some facial close-ups were added.

The chief's face conveyed great strength, from its lean muscularity and gleaming skin to its controlled, composed expression. This was the leader of a poor village struggling through difficult economic times. His face projected pride, determination, will, and an eagerness to be seen at his very best.

These are the moments that represent travel at its best, and we doubt they would have occurred without our desire to photograph the faces of the people we meet.

ABOVE. *A close-up meter reading of a person's face ensures the most accurate exposure for skin color. This particular gentleman enjoyed our attentions at a May Day celebration in Sienna, Italy.*

OPPOSITE. *To avoid a stiff and formal portrait, this young Ghanaian woman was posed against a dark wall, asked to turn away from the camera, and then to turn her head toward the photographer. The shot was taken at the instant of eye contact.*

Face to Face

No matter how interesting faces may be, portraits will succeed only if the skin tones are accurate. The main factors to consider are the actual skin color of the subject and the nature of the light.

Since faces may be many shades, they must be carefully metered for proper exposure. Be sure to meter the face itself, not the clothing, shawls, jewelry, or surroundings, which may be quite different in color and brightness from the skin. For the most accurate meter reading, move very close to the subject or use a hand-held spot meter.

The meter reading is a guide to proper exposure that must be tempered according to available light conditions. If at all possible, photograph the subject in the shade or in the uniformly diffused light of an overcast day. This will minimize harsh highlights, unflattering shadows on the face, and an unappealing squinty-eyed expression. Be aware of any colors cast within the shade by nearby walls, canopies, or foliage, which will change skin tonalities. If bright sun is unavoidable, try turning the subject away from the light source, using it for backlight or sidelight.

In diffused light or in bright sunshine, shoot at the meter reading for fair skin; underexpose up to one f-stop for very dark skin; and underexpose slightly—up to 1/2 stop—for skin tones in between. Bracket toward more underexposure with slide film. In dim light, such as is found in the deep shade of doorways, alleyways, covered markets, or at sunrise or sunset, overexposure may be needed. For light-skinned faces, overexpose up to one f-stop; for medium tones, overexpose up to 1/2 of an f-stop; and for dark skin, shoot at the meter reading. If the light is very dim, use your flash or switch to a high-speed film with an ISO of 400 and up.

Remember to pay attention to the background. For best results, look for a simple backdrop that creates a contrast of color and brightness with your subject.

Fleeting Expressions

The expression of painful determination on the sweaty face of this Senegalese palace guard was too arresting not to record.

Of all decisive moments the most engaging—and the most demanding—are those showing people's momentary facial expressions. These are the photographs that truly establish human connections, whether through humor, sympathy, or simple recognition. The challenge for the traveling photographer is to build those connections with people.

Because people who are not used to being photographed become somewhat self-conscious when a camera is up close, it is best to move back and use a moderate telephoto lens in the 85mm to 135mm range. But do not try to be invisible. You can respect the subject's right to be aware of being photographed without compromising the results. Trust is earned from knowing one's distance.

More vital than being out of sight is being out of mind. That is, the photographer's presence has to become unimportant to the subject. Naturally, this takes a little time. People do get used to the photographer after a few minutes, if they see no harm in what is being done and if the photographer has established rapport with them. Once the photographer is trusted and has been accepted as part of the scene, people tend to go about their business more naturally. That is when opportunities for capturing spontaneous expressions emerge.

But it takes concentration to watch people's ever-changing expressions. And it takes determination to anticipate what is about to happen and to be ready to photograph it. A boy's self-mocking grin, a couple's private exchange of intimacy, a palace guard's fleeting look of exhaustion, a musician's intense involvement in his craft: all these expressions can only be caught if we stalk them.

We recommend working in a limited area, choosing as a subject one person or one situation at a time. Trying to twist and turn in every direction because interesting things are going on is ultimately self-defeating. Fight the urge to capture everything in sight. And be prepared to take a series of shots, preferably with your strobe, because you can never be absolutely sure that you have gotten the one you have your heart set on.

Revealing Character

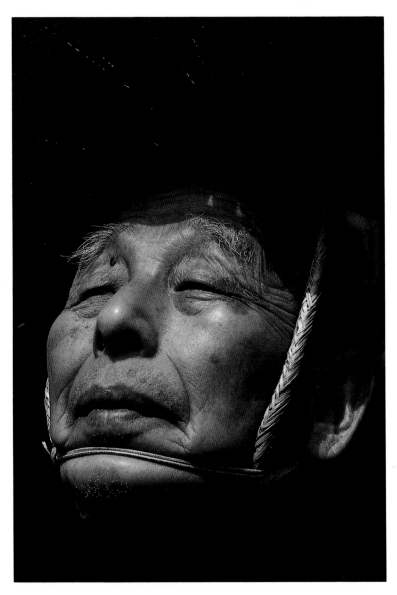

The shadows created by the large brim of the tightly bound, traditional hat worn by this Japanese gentleman accentuate the character of his face.

Faces appeal to us not only for their beauty but for their character. A face may project strength, poise, humor, wit, innocence, worldliness, suspicion, tenderness, or simply friendship. The character may reflect the personal qualities of our subject or some national or cultural trait.

The more clearly we can define what quality in a particular face interests us, the better are our chances of capturing that quality in our photographs. Here are some additional pointers to increase the likelihood of taking successful photographs:

1. Whether you are working with a normal, wide-angle, or telephoto lens, move in as close as seems comfortable. From a distance it is almost impossible to record character in people's faces.

2. Be relaxed and encourage your subject to relax. Chatting casually as you photograph helps the subject to have a natural expression. It takes a little time to get people used to being photographed at close range, so do not try to rush things.

3. As your subject gets used to you, introduce some gentle directions. Photographers of models achieve this by saying encouraging words, such as "That's it! That's perfect," or by giving some directions, "A little to the right." People seem truly flattered by the attention you give them in this process and try to please you. But be cognizant of the time when they are no longer enjoying the session. That is the time to stop and thank them profusely.

4. Involve your subject in decision-making. Ask your subject to assume a favorite pose or position, or see if the individual has a preference about where to stand or to sit. Ask if people want family, friends, or sentimental objects included, about which you may not know. This is a unique opportunity to personalize the photograph and to learn more about your subject.

5. Take shots from different directions. You never know which side of a person's face will prove to be the most evocative, so move around as you photograph.

ABOVE. *A child's love for a pet was captured when this boy snuggled close to his dogs in the back of his parents' pickup truck in Colorado.*

RIGHT. *This girl posed for us on her way back from one of Bali's numerous festivals, still wearing her beguiling costume, makeup, and floral tiara. A wide-angle lens sets her against the steep terrain.*

Enjoying Children

People around the world feel a palpable pride in their children. Consistently, when we photograph people, the parents want to bring their children into the picture. If the children are with them, they will call them over or hold them up or show them off in some other fashion. If the children are at home, people will offer to take us to their houses, so we can photograph their offspring. Similarly, if we start by taking photographs of the children, the adults are much more amenable to being photographed themselves.

Photographing children is one of the most challenging and demanding feats. The photographer must become immersed in the child's world, rather than trying to get the child to perform for the camera. The expressiveness in a child's face, however, makes it all worthwhile.

Here are some suggestions to keep in mind:

1. Children will not be still. Use a fast shutter speed of at least 1/125 of a second so fleeting movements and expressions can be caught at the decisive moment.
2. Work at the child's level. If that means getting down on the floor, do it. Look children in the eye to gain their trust.
3. Anything that saves time and energy helps: a motor drive, a zoom lens in the 35mm to 70mm range, automatic features for exposure and focus. Free yourself as much as possible to concentrate on the child's responses.
4. Talk softly and smile a lot. The age of your subject will determine the things you say, but even if you are speaking a language that is unintelligible to the child, keep the chatter going. Children will often mimic what you say, finding it strange and amusing. And smiling is universally understood and reassuring.
5. Enlist the assistance of nearby adults. They are usually more than pleased to help.

Dressed in his ceremonial robes and hat, this young Japanese boy exudes pleasure and pride.

ENVIRONMENTAL PORTRAITS

Another lovely way to create photographs of people we see in our travels is through environmental portraits. Unlike portraits, which focus on the face, and unlike action shots, which try to catch people at decisive moments, environmental portraits are designed to fuse subject and setting.

The setting may be their home, which reflects the condition of their lives—for better or worse—or their tastes and sensibilities. In other instances, the setting may be their place of work, complete with the tools of their trade. Or the environment may pertain to a leisure activity.

In composing environmental portraits, the photographer needs to balance carefully the subject and the setting. The people must be visually dominant so their surroundings do not overpower or diminish them. On the other hand, the settings must be clearly visible and frame the people in a meaningful way.

Because the relationship between the subject and the environment is so vital, and since you will want to produce sharp pictures that are also well exposed, use a small aperture of f/8 or higher, and try to shoot with uniform light throughout. Any major light differences—2 f-stops or more—will essentially destroy the effect of this kind of composition.

It is possible to take an environmental portrait as a candid shot, while the subject is engaged in an activity. But it is just as effective, and often less time consuming and frustrating, to pose the subject. The pose, however, should be relaxed and informal.

Plan the photograph with your subjects before you start shooting and feel free to discuss possible poses and placements with them. Whatever you decide, remember to consider the effect of light on your results, both indoors and outdoors. And assert your judgment about the way the background sets off your subject. After all, it is the person who caught your eye.

For proper exposure of this environmental portrait of a Buddhist monk sitting at the entrance to a small neighborhood shrine in Takayama, Japan, the wall was metered and underexposed by half a stop.

Indoors

Indoor environmental portraits present their own opportunities and difficulties. On the plus side, they give traveling photographers a chance to show people inside their homes, shops, places of worship, restaurants, and places of entertainment or amusement. But interior spaces are not nearly as brightly lit as the outdoors, presenting the problems of maintaining sharpness and proper exposure under dim light. Therefore, fast film, slow shutter speeds, or electronic flash will be needed.

Unless you are using a tripod, use film that is rated at least

ISO 200. Meter your subject's face and select an exposure setting that allows for the smallest possible aperture to maximize sharpness. But remember that with a slower shutter speed, the camera and subject will have to be increasingly steady.

Electronic flash for indoor environmental portraits works best for providing fill-in light. Since the flash will only illuminate the foreground subject and, perhaps, a few feet of the backdrop, anything more than 10 feet (3 m) away from the camera will be lost in darkness. If the background is close behind the subject, the flash unit may be able to illuminate both. Otherwise, meter and expose for the backdrop environment, allowing light to accumulate on the film with a slow shutter speed. Then, with the flash unit on "fill-in" mode, set the compensation dial to underexpose from 1/2 to 1 full stop.

Another consideration when photographing an indoor environmental portrait is the type of interior lighting being used. Different light sources produce different colors. Unless the photographer uses film balanced for the specific light source, the color will affect people's skin tones. That may or may not be objectionable. The reddish glow of candlelight or the orange color of incandescent light may be perfectly acceptable. But the greenish cast of fluorescent lights may not be especially flattering or desirable.

An alternative to changing film with each circumstance is using color correction filters with the daylight film in your camera. These special filters screw onto the front of the lens to neutralize undesirable colors. Or use fill-in flash, which provides a burst of white light similar to daylight.

A wide-angle lens is a real boon for composing indoors. It allows the photographer to work in cramped interiors such as shops, markets, and restaurants.

A wide-angle lens portrays the receptionists at our hotel in Bali within the setting of the beautifully crafted open-air lobby where we first saw them.

Outdoors

Outdoor environmental portraits are a favorite way of photographing travel companions, and they can also expand our travel shots of local people. No matter who the people may be, the challenge in these portraits is to find the right balance between the subject and the setting.

In part the difficulty derives from the contrast of size and scale between the two key elements. Outdoor space is larger than we realize, not only in a panoramic landscape but in market, harbor, village, or city street. Framing a person in such a vast space is problematic, especially if we want the human dimension to be dominant. The tendency is to overplay one element or the other: a tiny person against a panoramic view, or a portrait that blocks the surroundings.

Ideally the composition features the person and allows the setting to complement the portrait. A normal lens may be too restrictive for such a combination, because it forces the photographer to move back to frame the person and the background subjects together. However, with the person so far removed, the resulting image ceases to be a true portrait.

A moderate wide-angle lens, in the 35mm to 28mm range, can solve this dilemma, since it allows the photographer to move close to the subject, so that the person whose portrait is being taken can remain prominent in the foreground. At the same time, its broad perspective captures the surroundings more fully than a normal lens would at the same distance.

A low perspective shows this Egyptian gatekeeper standing with his key before the colossal figures at Abu Simbel. A small aperture retains a sharp background.

Another challenge is that outdoor photography is done mostly with available light, and not all light will be equally flattering to your subject. Uniform light is easiest to work with because both subject and background are evenly lit, avoiding harsh contrasts of bright and dark. Uniform light also makes successful exposure and composition simpler.

In bright light, place the subject in the highlighted area and expose for the person's face, whether it is turned toward or away from the light source. Exposure on the face should be given priority, even if the background is over- or underexposed to some extent. Neutralize any unsightly shadows on the subject's face with fill-in flash.

Outdoor environmental portraits offer the great advantage of increased flexibility: the photographer or the subject can readily move or turn in a direction that produces the best composition or lighting. Experiment with asymmetrical arrangements where the subject is not dead center or staring straight into the camera. And look for lines in the environment—trails, coastlines, roads, pavements—that draw the eye into the photograph and create the illusion of depth.

Wearing his full regalia, a village chief in northern Ghana is shown against the background of his family compound.

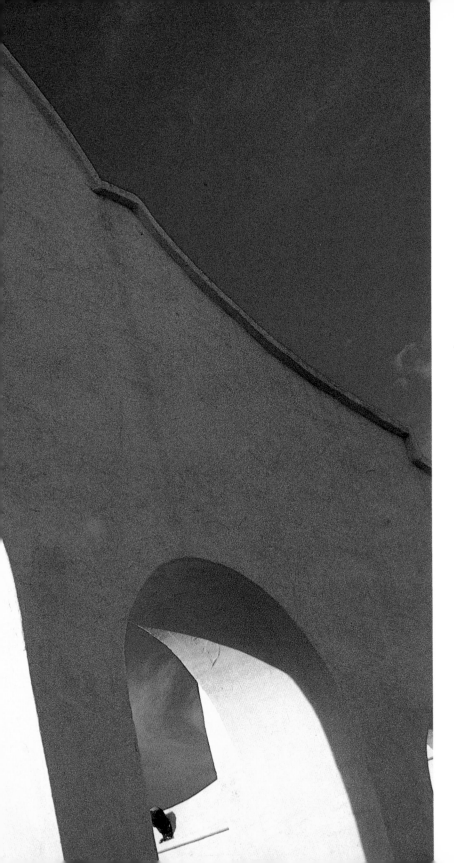

7
Architecture

"... his [Frederick Evans] cathedral pictures were photographs not of stone but of space."

JOHN SZARKOWSKI, 1973

BUILDING STYLE

One of the most compelling reasons to travel is to see the architectural wonders of the world from ancient structures to recent engineering marvels. We derive a strong sense of history from seeing magnificent artifacts from a different time. And since so many of these relics of the past were made of stone, they survived through the centuries, now serving as reminders of human ingenuity and determination.

To historians, buildings from previous eras reveal a wealth of cultural information about how people lived and worked and what they believed in. The pyramids of ancient Egypt, the cathedrals of medieval Europe, and the skyscrapers of modern North America provide us with knowledge about three very different societies.

These architectural masterpieces draw us to distant lands. We want to see them for ourselves and to photograph them. From the earliest years of photography, the camera has been used to document these monuments of civilization.

Yet it is also evident that simple structures are worthy of our attention. In addition to famous temples, fabled castles, and wondrous antiquities, typical homes of everyday people are equally fascinating. These plain houses are naturally less notable than the edifices left by powerful

PAGES 172–173. *Travelers can photograph architecture in a documentary fashion or attempt more personal interpretations of buildings around the world, as in this image of the San Xavier Mission outside Tucson, Arizona. The church is viewed through its entrance arches, dramatically set against a deep blue sky.*

LEFT. *Part of a large building may give a clearer sense of its style than a picture of the whole. One section of the Heian Shrine in Kyoto, Japan, suggests the structure's symmetrical plan, vermilion exterior, and tiled roof.*

rulers, but they provide a meaningful cultural commentary of their own.

Photographically speaking, architecture has the advantage of standing still. We do not have to rush or use fast shutter speeds. We can take our time to walk around them, compose carefully, and look for unusual vantage points. On the other hand, there may be difficulties related to their size, scale, and possible distortion. The following pages will show you how to look at architecture with a camera and come back with memorable results.

ABOVE. *Castles photographed at close range are often too large to fit into the frame. A perspective from a nearby hill shows the entire castle of Mad King Ludwig, together with its Bavarian mountaintop setting, in a flattering late afternoon light.*

LEFT. *An unusual wide-angle image of Turkey's Hagia Sophia mosque combines the enormous Byzantine structure with a small building nearby, its protruding black roof looming above.*

Skyscrapers

Through the ages, one of the measures of architectural achievement has been size. The sheer dimensions of a temple or palace announced the wealth and power of the state and its rulers. In a sense, this is still true: an architectural hallmark of the modern city is often its skyscrapers, symbolizing advances in technology and wealth. A tradition that may have begun as a brazen act with the Tower of Babel has continued into the twentieth century with the Eiffel Tower, the Empire State Building, and numerous other buildings of enormous height.

There are a variety of excellent ways to include tall structures within the picture frame:

1. Shoot the skyline. From a sufficient distance, the skyline of a city can include numerous tall buildings, a composite that may evoke the mood of the city better than that of a single building. Use a telephoto lens in the 80mm to 200mm range to bring the skyline closer and to compress the space between buildings.
2. Shoot from another skyscraper. Some fine overviews of the city can be taken from the observation decks provided by many skyscrapers. Unfortunately, a city can look flat and dull from a very high perspective. Including other tall buildings helps establish a better sense of scale.

TOP. *An unobstructed view of the lower Manhattan skyline is seen from Liberty State Park in New Jersey. Daylight film turns fluorescent lights green, tungsten lights orange, and the sky black.*

LEFT. *San Francisco's Transamerica Building is shown as a reflection on the shiny glass exterior of a nearby skyscraper. The camera's position was critical to organize all the lines to meet at an unseen vanishing point. Meter the sky and underexpose by half a stop.*

Depending on the distance between skyscrapers, anything from a normal 50mm lens to a moderate 100mm lens should make such a photograph possible.

3. Shoot looking up. This is what many travelers do spontaneously—or try to do—only to find that the skyscraper is just too tall. You will probably need a wide-angle lens of 28mm or wider to get most of a tall building from below. Use your vertical format and give priority to the top, which draws the eye skyward and is often distinctive. Or frame the shot to include a dramatic foreground object, such as a large or colorful sculpture in the ground-level plaza.

4. Shoot at night. All of the above suggestions work just as well, and sometimes better, at night. Skyscrapers are often lit by special floodlights at night, adding color to the picture. Even if they are not illuminated, the lights of offices in their towers record well with a slow shutter speed of a few seconds or more, depending on the amount of available light. To ensure a good exposure, take several shots, increasing exposure times by the original number of seconds each time. Use a tripod, or rest your camera on a stationary ledge to keep it absolutely steady.

5. Shoot abstractions. Use the lines, shapes, and architectural details of the skyscraper to create interesting abstractions. Also, look for partial views of tall buildings wedged among other typical city elements or reflected in nearby windows or shiny walls. These can convey the high-tech look of the building or the cacophonous quality of city life.

The towers of San Francisco's Golden Gate Bridge loom skyward when photographed from Fort Point below. To enhance the color of the bridge, the sky was metered and underexposed by half a stop, and an 81A warming filter was added.

Castles, Temples, and Cathedrals

On a lower order of magnitude, though not of magnificence, are the legendary edifices of faith and fortitude built through the ages. Pilgrims of the past, who undertook long journeys inspired by religious fervor or the need for protection, have been supplanted by today's travelers, in search of a closer look at the world's architectural riches.

For the traveling photographer, castles, temples, and cathedrals are intriguing, almost magical subjects. The challenge is to photograph them in a meaningful and original way. Begin by allowing some time to explore the site. One cannot absorb history instantaneously; nor does one appreciate such intricate structures in a straightforward way. Undoubtedly, there are surprising corners to turn and numerous vantage points to discover—from below, above, or nearby.

Here is the perfect opportunity to apply an earlier lesson: start with some overviews, move in for a closer perspective, then find those telling details that make the experience most personal.

The overview can show the entire building, including its setting, whether a mountaintop, a garden, or a busy city. Before you arrive at your destination begin to think about the overview, so you can scout out interesting directions and angles. You may need to climb to the roof, turret, or nearby hillside to show the structure with its surroundings.

The middle ground can take advantage of such architectural frames as arcades, gates, and doorways, using a wide-angle lens to emphasize the sense of depth and distance. Since buildings of this size are too large to fit within the frame at a close distance, look for partial views that capture the essence of the structure's space and style, utilizing shapes, forms, and shadows to help organize the composition.

Finally, if possible, return to photograph these structures early or late in the day, so that the effects of softer light can be used.

The distinctive shape of this Turkish mosque in Istanbul is dramatically revealed in silhouette against a sunset. A slight underexposure of the sky enriched the colors, and a powerful telephoto lens isolated the structure from its distracting surroundings.

Antiquities and Monuments

There is another kind of architecture, similar in scale to some castles, temples, or cathedrals, but quite different to experience and photograph. These are structures that have ceased to have a life and utility of their own except to represent huge museum pieces or commemorative markers.

As travelers, we value them as reminders of ancient civilizations or of events that we wish to retain in our collective memories. They often puzzle and amaze us with their beauty, craftsmanship, and endurance, reflecting as they do the most splendid tribute to their times. They may stir feelings of sorrow, patriotism, or shame, as they recall the cycles of natural destruction and war.

As photographers we hope to convey not only what we see but what we feel. We want to translate our understanding and appreciation in visual terms, by highlighting the unique qualities of each site. For the ruins of the past, whether in Egypt, Greece, Rome, Latin America, or elsewhere, evoke a complex set of emotions. Our task is to identify those emotions honestly and transmit them through our images.

A few technical pointers may be helpful:
1. When shooting in very bright daylight, make deep shadows part of your composition, and use a polarizing filter to remove glare and reflections or to deepen a blue sky. Also, try shooting early or late in the day, or even at night, when many monuments are illuminated.
2. Use people or familiar objects to provide a sense of scale. Some of the vast ancient statuary and columns are hard to imagine without a measure of comparison.
3. A wide-angle lens is invaluable for taking in broad or tall architectural elements, and for combining foreground subjects with the architectural setting.
4. A telephoto lens can help isolate details such as carvings, reliefs, or statuary.

TOP. *Many antiquities and monuments are illuminated at night. Here the Great Pyramid in Giza, Egypt, is viewed from a distance using a long exposure of 5 minutes to produce the backlit radiating effect. Many exposures were taken at 15- to 90-second increments to guarantee a usable image, since it was too dark to obtain a meter reading.*

ABOVE. *Finding new ways to portray famous monuments takes imagination and effort. Here three flags were incorporated in a wide-angle shot of the Washington Monument.*

Humble Abodes

While grand architecture may inspire our travels, often more humble structures charm us. As traveling photographers we should not neglect them in our picture-taking.

Look for buildings that use typical designs and materials for the region: the thatched cottages of the Cotswolds; the brownstones of New York City; the smooth, mud-walled compounds of West Africa; the canal houses of Amsterdam or Venice; the clusters of painted adobe houses found throughout the Mediterranean.

To add variety and interest to these images, avoid the mug shots taken by real estate agents. Come in close enough so that the character of the home shines through. A normal to moderate telephoto lens up to 100mm should allow you to include the setting, whether it is a garden, a street, a canal, or the countryside.

Compose your photographs for maximum clarity and simplicity, eliminating anything that would detract from your image. Be careful not to give too much visual space to unneeded foreground elements, such as lawns, trees, and fences. Notice such distractions as wires, parked cars, or garbage cans, and change your perspective to remove them from your image.

Do display distinctive architectural features, such as interesting roofs, stonework, or doorways. Simple domestic touches may also be part of your composition: hanging laundry, a bicycle leaning against a wall, a rocking chair on the porch all comment on the lives of the occupants of the house. Just be sure to use these objects as graphic components in your composition.

And, of course, if the family is around, do not be embarrassed by your attention to their home. Tell them how much

An abandoned farmhouse in North Dakota glows with a fiery red of the setting sun. The red reflected from the interior was metered and underexposed one stop.

you admire it, ask them questions about the house, and see if they would agree to pose in a photograph of it. If they are receptive, you may get to see other parts of the house that would otherwise have been off-limits. You may even be asked inside, opening yet another door to photographic possibilities.

RIGHT. *A caretaker's "cottage" on the grounds of Versailles was photographed from across a pond using a soft-focus filter.*

BELOW. *Laundry hanging in a courtyard mimics the technicolor houses of Burano, Italy.*

Architectural Details

The smaller architectural elements of a structure may reveal as much character as the grand design. A door, a window, a roof, a gate or tower, even a set of steps can be exciting.

These details do not have to be perfect specimens of taste or workmanship to warrant our attention. An old, weathered barn door may spark our imaginations as readily as the well-crafted portal of a palace.

In photographing architectural details it is important to remember to make the image large enough so that the subject is shown in its full glory. That means either getting close or using a telephoto lens in the 100mm to 200mm range.

The following pointers should also be useful:

1. Emphasize shape. Details such as doors and windows often have very alluring shapes: arches, pointed arches, or gables. Show these off by creating a framework around the shape or by using the shape as a silhouette and photographing through the opening to record what is beyond the door or window. Remember to meter through the opening so the scene beyond is well exposed.

2. Look for texture. Building materials are often highly textured, adding an interesting dimension to photographs of architecture. Roofs, for instance, can be tiled, leaded, or thatched, each yielding a very different effect. Walls may be stone, wood, stucco, or painted adobe. Juxtapose a structure's contrasting materials. Light that casts shadows to the side brings out textures.

3. Discover patterns and rhythms. Architectural details often come in recurring sets, creating a rhythmic visual flow. Think of an arcade of arches, a forest of columns, a row of doorways, a cascade of steps.

TOP. *A window detail reveals delicate filigree designs carved in stone on the facade of Jodhpur's Meherangarh Fort.*

ABOVE. *Small windows keep the mud-brick huts of northern Ghana cool. The women of the compound create and paint the geometric designs on the outside walls.*

Sculpture

Three-dimensional art has long played an important role in conjunction with architecture. Ancient temples were richly decorated with relief sculpture depicting stories of conquest and of gods and rulers. Low- and high-relief carvings were augmented with statuary, some still restrained by church and temple walls, others fully liberated as freestanding sculpture. Today enormous modern sculptures grace the plazas in front of austere modern office buildings.

For traveling photographers, the interplay of architectural forms and statuary is both interesting and challenging, with three key issues to consider:

1. Should the architecture and statuary be visually integrated or separated? A casual or thoughtless approach to this issue will result in a muddled, poorly defined image. To achieve an integrated image, use a small aperture and possibly a wide-angle lens for maximum depth of field. To separate the architectural background from the statuary, keep the depth of field shallow with a normal or telephoto lens. Also, use high-contrast light by moving until the sculpture is set against a shadow and expose for the well-lit subject.

2. What is the best perspective for the image? A low perspective, taken from the ground and shooting upward, allows us to combine near and distant subjects, such as a plaza sculpture and a skyscraper. But shooting the statuary over the cathedral portals may require a higher vantage point, which may not always be possible.

3. How does lighting affect the image? The play of light on the highly textured surface of statuary is a crucial element in making these sculptural forms come to life. Determine the times of day when the light will fall on the statuary most effectively, both in terms of color and direction. The extremes of the day are often most flattering. Avoid flat, frontal light for textural interest and sculptural depth.

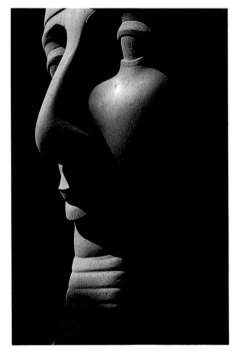

ABOVE. *A floodlit statuary, like this one in Florence's Fountain of Neptune, becomes especially dramatic if photographed with daylight film.*

LEFT. *This Egyptian sculpture located deep within an ancient tomb near Luxor was illuminated with natural sunlight that is ingeniously reflected with mirrors.*

INTERIORS

Especially in cities, a great deal of travel time is spent indoors. With the wish to record the highlights of their trip, the majority of traveling photographers succumb to the temptation to whip out their cameras and start snapping interiors. Invariably, the resulting photographs are dismal disappointments.

Too many photographers rely on their flash to provide the needed light for interior shots. Flash units, even if they are quite powerful, can only reach so far, generally no more than 15 to 20 feet (5 to 7 meters). They can never provide uniform illumination throughout an interior: the forward areas will always be brighter than those farther away.

A flash simply will not do the job of lighting up the nave

of a cathedral or a vast domed ceiling. These cavernous interiors, though worthy photographic subjects, can only be adequately captured by using a slow exposure, so that light can accumulate on the film for at least several seconds.

Even in the more confined spaces of museums and historic homes, a flash will splash the area with a burst of bright light, often creating hot spots off reflective surfaces. The new electronic cameras are better at regulating the light output for single objects, such as a sculpture or work of art, although they lack the ability to produce the soft, uniform illumination professionals want in photographing art. But for room settings, where objects fill an area of some depth, the most sophisticated flash units will be inadequate.

If this sounds discouraging, it is meant to be. It takes a special effort to produce good pictures of interiors. In particular, it means using a tripod, so the camera can remain steady for a long exposure. It also often means getting permission in advance to take photographs, especially with a tripod.

For those willing to make such an effort, this section will show you how to achieve satisfying results, even in the relative rush of a travel experience. For those who prefer not to bother—and we sympathize completely—you may wish to check the local shop for postcards or transparencies of the interior scenes or objects of greatest interest to you.

Photographing interiors requires careful composition and long exposures as well as the use of a tripod. The graceful vault and delicate stained-glass windows of Paris's Sainte-Chapelle required an extreme wide-angle lens and a 4-second exposure.

Museums and Rotundas

The sensation of standing in a vast enclosed space is often more thrilling than seeing the exterior structure that defines that space.

Here are some suggestions to help you convey the grandeur of these interiors:

1. Rely on a wide-angle lens. A 28mm to 24mm lens can portray vast interior spaces. There will be some distortion, with parallel lines tending to converge or bend toward one another. Only specialized perspective control lenses can avoid this problem.

2. Compose using symmetry. Unless a space is decidedly modern, it will be organized in a balanced, symmetrical way. Take advantage of the architect's plan by using that order. Think in terms of the columns, arches, arcades, staircases, and pediments that define the space. Shoot straight up at ceilings, or through arcades, aligning the architectural forms for visual balance.

3. Expose for the dark areas. Most interiors are quite dim. The film's capacity to accumulate light makes it possible to brighten and reveal color, well beyond what the eye can see. By exposing for the darker areas, preferably using a spot meter, and bracketing toward overexposure, interiors can take on jewellike clarity. Including candles or chandeliers adds lovely highlights and color contrasts within the image.

4. Use the smallest aperture for maximum sharpness. A very slow shutter speed will require camera stability, preferably on a tripod. However, photographers have used banisters, ledges, and floors to support cameras during long exposures. The tripod, however, gives the photographer the greatest compositional flexibility and control. An added bonus of the slow shutter speed is that people in motion will effectively vanish.

TOP. *Without a tripod, a camera can be kept motionless by resting it on the floor and using a self-timer, as in this photograph taken in the Chinese Pavilion at Disneyworld in Florida.*

ABOVE. *A symmetrical composition taken in Amsterdam's Rijksmuseum required a very steady hand since a long shutter speed was needed and the use of a tripod was not allowed.*

Decor and Art

Photographing vast interior spaces, such as in this rococo church—the Wieskirche in Bavaria—requires a wide-angle lens and a tripod for a long exposure.

Photographing more decorative interiors, such as those in historic houses, royal palaces, and people's homes, requires many of the same techniques used in more public buildings.

There are a few additional ideas the traveling photographer would do well to consider:

1. Compose with a point of interest in mind. Rooms photographed haphazardly tend not to engage the viewer. Find the focal point the designer or owner may have had in mind for the room—a canopy bed, a huge table, walls hung with tapestries. Or select something that interests you. Usually there is much to choose from among the furnishings, textiles, and wall and floor coverings. Whatever your point of interest, have it dominate the visual space of your photograph.
2. Expose with purpose. Meter the items of most importance to you, as well as the dark areas of the room. Compromises may have to be made if the light is not sufficiently uniform. If so, favor proper exposure on what really matters to you, allowing other parts of the room to be underexposed, if necessary.
3. Maximize sharpness. Use a small aperture and a tripod to stabilize the camera during long exposures.
4. Have filters handy. A polarizing filter helps remove hot spots and reflections from mirrors or glossy floors and furnishings. Color correction filters may be needed if daylight film is in the camera but indoor lights are illuminating the scene. Otherwise, incandescent (tungsten) lights will create a warm, orange glow, while fluorescent lights will produce a greenish cast.

LOOKING THROUGH GLASS

Glass is both a joy and a nuisance to photograph. It has three wonderful properties that captivate the imagination and have the potential to transform the mundane into the magical. These same properties, however, can also be frustrating aspects of the material.

The first appealing property of glass is its transparency. In fact, photographers are so taken by their ability to see through glass that they forget it is there. That is when glass begins to play its tricks on us, luring us into photographic traps. For example, we fail to notice reflections that interfere with our ability to portray what interests us on the other side. Sometimes we even activate our flash units, forgetting that the bright light will bounce right back at us. There are marvelous things we can photograph through windows, museum dioramas, aquarium glass, and shop displays. But we will have to be objective in our looking and scrupulously obey certain precautions.

A second enchanting quality of glass is its reflectivity. While reflections are not always noticed or wanted, they can become subjects in their own right. The sheen of a modern glass office tower can mirror all sorts of interesting city sights, sometimes with abstract twists and distortions. Reflections can also be incorporated as partial images, in combination with whatever lurks on the other side of the glass, to create highly individual interpretations of the surroundings.

Finally, the translucency of glass has made it ideal for the inspired creations of stained glass artists through the ages. The magnificent windows of Europe's medieval cathedrals draw crowds to this day, and other examples of decorative touches of stained glass abound in architecture around the world.

Our task as photographers is to learn how to make the properties of glass serve our vision and purpose.

Looking through the window of a typical New York City delicatessen reveals the foods and workers inside. The neon sign and some reflections of a street scene add interest to the shot.

Windows and Displays

A few simple precautions will produce the results you expect when photographing through the glass of windows and displays. All too often, photographers shoot through glass as if they were shooting through air.

A few suggestions:
1. Move close to the subject. By standing close to the glass surface, you will reduce reflections that will interfere with your picture. The lens can even touch the glass, preferably with a collapsible rubber lens shade as a buffer.
2. Do not use a flash. The light will only bounce off the glass, leaving a bright glare spot and little else. If the display is dimly lit, steady the camera on a tripod or nearby ledge and take as long an exposure as necessary.
3. Polarize. Use a polarizing filter to eliminate reflections when you cannot move close enough, or if you are forced to shoot at an angle that retains some reflections. If you want some, but not all of the reflections, watch carefully through the lens as you rotate the polarizing filter, and turn it to just the point that satisfies you. Of course, if the reflections interest you, be sure you are not polarizing them out of the photograph.
4. Use a wide-angle lens. Most scenes beyond the glass are still in fairly confined quarters. The wide-angle lens takes in a broader expanse than other lenses.

Remember that besides aquariums and museums where you are on the outside looking in, there are possibilities for shooting on the inside looking out, such as observing the street scene outside a window.

Special care is neeed for looking through glass with both the inside and outside in good exposure. This is best accomplished if the light differential between the two sides is no more than three f-stops.

The transparency of glass made it possible to combine a vase of tulips on a windowsill with the Dutch flag waving outside into an interesting composition based on color affinities. If more light is needed to balance the exposure between the interior and exterior, a reflector or carefully positioned fill-in flash can provide it.

Stained Glass

With all its gemlike beauty stained glass is not difficult to photograph. The problems photographers do encounter are quite simple to remedy.

The first difficulty arises from a misunderstanding about which way to point the camera. Our eyes tend to turn spontaneously toward the brightest point. Often that is where the sun is shining. While our eyes can accommodate the disparity in light between highlights and the more subdued areas, we often forget that film—especially slide film—has less latitude. If we aim the camera toward the sun, the photograph will be exposed for the bright spot, leaving the surroundings much dimmer and effectively spoiling the luminescence of the stained glass.

A more satisfying photograph can be made by using uniform light. That is why bright, overcast light works more successfully than intense sunshine for shooting stained glass. If you happen to be at the location on a sunny day, aim your camera toward the side away from or opposite the sun to achieve a uniform effect.

Proper exposure is also something of a problem. When they photograph stained glass most people envision a photo with jewellike clarity and richness of color. However, the many colors of stained glass may require different exposures for true rendition. Meter the middle tones and, if possible, use a spot meter on those areas. Then bracket toward overexposure to brighten the colors further. With autoexposure cameras, set the exposure compensation dial to +1/2, +1 and +1 1/2 to achieve overexposure. Use your smallest aperture to maximize sharpness and clarity. If a slow shutter speed is needed, steady your camera on a tripod or other brace.

Finally, compose your image so it makes sense of the stained glass. If you are photographing an entire chapel area, be sure it reflects the architectural order or symmetry. For details use a telephoto lens to isolate scenes from the whole.

To retain true, rich colors in bright backlight, it is wise to take several exposures at slightly different settings, as in this detail of a stained-glass window in a synagogue in Tucson, Arizona.

8
In Action

*"For me the camera is a sketch book,
an instrument of intuition and spontaneity,
the master of the instant . . ."*

HENRI CARTIER BRESSON, 1976

SHOOTING ON THE MOVE

At a time when many people travel with video cameras, we may ask why recording any action shots with a still camera is desirable. Our answer is that still photography transforms movement into images that go far beyond the visible instant, as we saw it, or as it would appear in a moving medium such as video.

PAGES 190-191. *To children, the Great Sand Dunes of Colorado are an enormous sandbox. A favorite activity is leaping over the dunes, caught here using a wide-angle lens and a fast shutter speed.*

ABOVE. *As this cowboy rides in a Colorado rodeo the sensation of movement is created by deliberately blurring the image at a slow shutter speed. Premetering the ground ensured accurate exposure under unpredictable conditions.*

The feature that most distinguishes still from motion photography (including video) is the photographer's ability to control the variable of time. Most still cameras have a range of shutter speeds, from 1 second to 1/500 of a second, with many models extending this range in both directions.

The slower the shutter speed, the more blurred the moving subject will be. When the blur is just right, it evokes the excitement of the moment, recreating the action through sensation rather than clarity. An example of this approach is a photograph at a rodeo of a cowboy galloping on his horse: the tension of the ride would not be conveyed as powerfully if the image were absolutely sharp.

On the other hand, a fast shutter speed—sometimes supplemented with an electronic flash—captures a fleeting instant in time. Harold Edgerton, the master of such freeze-frame photography, showed us the beauty of the most ordinary actions, such as a drop of milk landing on a dish. Similarly, the photograph of a little boy jumping over a sand dune catches him at the peak of his leap, sharply and crisply, with an immediacy no moving medium can match.

In both cases, the desired image is partly the result of careful planning and preparation, and partly a matter of luck. Some people depend on luck and simply fire away rapidly. The resulting photographs—essentially a progression of steps in the entire motion—may contain some gems. But the likelihood of photographic success in action will increase greatly by making the most of what a still camera can do.

People on the Go

Wherever you travel, you will see people on the go: people at work, at play, celebrating, and strolling. The photographer with the ambition to capture the spirit of a trip will want to show some of these activities.

To do so, we recommend taking the following approaches:

1. Take a watch-and-see attitude. Find an observation spot. Decide to stay put while you savor the rhythm of daily activities. This will give you a chance to develop your timing. Children cavorting at an amusement park, cruise ship passengers dancing, or ordinary street life take on a fascinating aura when viewed as potential action shots.

2. Search for local rhythms. Look for routines in every culture. These may be seasonal, such as harvesting; weekly, such as going to market; or daily, such as preparing meals. These repeated activities are a rich pictorial resource. We once found such photographic inspiration in an Arab village where a woman was sifting grains of wheat. We saw that she sifted wheat with a back and forth movement, then tossed it up. After noticing this pattern, we shot the picture the instant the wheat grains were in the air.

3. Include your travel companions in action shots. While portraying local people engaged in unfamiliar activities is a challenge for any photographer, catching your friends and family doing something spontaneous will also enliven your photo collection in a very personal way.

To stop the action, use the fastest possible shutter speed or an electronic flash unit. Even in daylight, the burst of light from the flash will freeze the motion and keep the picture sharp.

Keep in mind what you are most interested in visualizing. If expression and movement are foremost, get reasonably close to your subject and isolate the action. If the action is interesting because of its context, show the setting in a meaningful way.

TOP. *Children in Ghana are often sent to fetch water from the town pump. As these children sang and danced along a road on the outskirts of Accra, their animated figures formed silhouettes against a sky at sunset.*

ABOVE. *A telling moment was captured on film when a high-spirited New York shopper twirled to model a dress for her companion to admire.*

From Planes, Trains, and Automobiles

The movement essential to all travel is the one that transports the traveler from one place to another. As we fly, chug, drive, or float from one destination to another, we view fascinating sights. And considering how much time we spend in transport, and how much looking we do while en route, it is worthwhile to think of these moments as opportunities for picture-taking.

For example, people routinely "ooh" and "ah" as they look from airplanes to the scenes below. While many photographers are discouraged from photographing in the air by the prospect of having to shoot through the planes' scratched

To neutralize the vibrations of our seaplane, this aerial shot of Alaska's Misty Fjords was taken at the fastest possible shutter speed, with the camera braced against the photographer's body and with the focus preset at infinity.

plastic windows, it turns out that these windows are not such great impediments after all. On a flight to Denver in 1979, we discovered that the windows' mylar coating coupled with a polarizing filter create psychedelic colors on bodies of water. To recreate this effect, set a lens fitted with a polarizer directly against the window. By turning the polarizer, the colors change as if through a kaleidoscope. In smaller aircraft, where windows are likely to be even more marred, neutralize this distraction by using a moderate telephoto lens—80mm to 200mm—and by bracing it against the window.

Since the airplane is high above the subject, its movement is not a major factor in picture-taking, but work quickly before the landscape passes from view. To eliminate the effect of the plane's vibration, shoot at a fast shutter speed—1/250 of a second or faster.

Photographing during a car trip has become easier since scenic turnouts have been made for travelers in many parts of the world. While these views are often spectacular, they can become rather trite. Instead try a detour along smaller highways where stops are possible for more original shots.

Plan your trip with enough time to stop and photograph wonderful views. The momentum of the car and the necessity to move on are powerful deterrents to roadside photography. If taking pictures is important to you, then you will have to overcome the natural reluctance to pull over.

Do not assume that a more beautiful spot will be down the road, and do not take chances on photographing from the car. The normal speed of a moving car causes anything in the foreground to be blurred. Distant subjects may be sharp if shot at 1/500 of a second or faster, but they are not likely to be well composed. In addition, when you photograph from a car, distracting objects, such as telephone poles, may interfere with the scenery.

Even so, there are special cases when shooting from inside

a car may be worthwhile, especially if you want to convey the sensation of the ride, not the scene beyond. During a stay at Coral Pink Sand Dunes in Utah, we were invited to ride in a dune buggy, a first experience of this sort for us. Naturally, we wanted to take pictures as we careened in the vehicle, churning up sand and dust. The hard part was letting go of the handles long enough to lift the camera, aim, and shoot. This was a time for luck to play its part.

Most boat rides are comparatively slow, giving the photographer some time to compose and plan each shot while moving. Use a fast shutter speed—at least 1/60 of a second—if movement is noticeable. Since it is not possible to get off the boat, integrate it into your view of the general scene.

A final point on photographing as you move from place to place: include pictures of your means of transportation. Whether it is a highway, a river, a railroad track, or the sky itself, showing how you got from here to there can enliven your travel pictures in a very personal way.

TOP. *A zoom lens helps compose initial impressions as a ship comes into the port of Thíra (Santorini) in Greece. Control potential vibrations by using a fast shutter speed.*

RIGHT. *Taking a camera along on a dune buggy ride at Coral Pink Sand Dunes State Park in Utah proved daring but worthwhile. In the frame a part of the vehicle offers a point of reference, and a fast shutter speed stops motion.*

Parades

Every country has its holidays and festivals, many of which are celebrated with parades. American parades tend to be relatively spectacular affairs, with floats, flags, bands, baton twirlers, and balloons. The spontaneity and fervor of the audience is often as interesting as the main event, especially the wide-eyed expressions of children watching a parade for the first time.

Our own tastes tend to run toward the less slick, but more expressive, parades we have come upon in Africa and Asia. On a trip to Ghana we happened to be in the area of Mepe when

a gathering of local clans was taking place, complete with a huge parade. We had no idea what to expect. As the drumbeats echoed everywhere, the crowds poured into the narrow main street of the town. Suddenly, a sea of people dressed in red clothing danced and sang their way down the street. We scrambled to find a spot from which to see well and managed to climb on a truck with a platform. From this vantage point, we could photograph without being jostled and pushed by those on the ground. At strategic moments, they rose and danced, waving symbols of power to their clanspeople. Then the queen passed below us, stately and regal in her robes and shielded by an enormous ceremonial umbrella. It was thrilling from start to finish.

The same sense of bewildering excitement swept over us in Bali, when we came upon one of the nearly daily parades held on this lovely Indonesian island. This orderly procession was punctuated with the appearance of remarkable giant icons from the Hindu pantheon. Again, we found ourselves so overwhelmed, we hardly knew which way to turn.

Undoubtedly, you will have a similar experience of not knowing whether to watch the parade or to occupy yourself photographing it.

If you love parades, we have a few pointers for you:
1. Work around the crowd. Be bold if you want to take pictures from the right place. Do not get discouraged, and be prepared to be jostled and perhaps to jostle back.
2. Look before you shoot. Get a sense of what will be happening so you can be ready. Alternate between looking through your camera and surveying the actual scene to spot spectacles that have not yet reached you. If possible, work with a partner who can scout for opportunities.
3. Simplify your equipment. Use a zoom lens—28mm to 135mm—to compose quickly. Rely on automatic features for exposure and focus, and go for snapshots. Or preset your nonautomatic camera and wait for your chosen subject to enter your frame.

4. Vary your perspective. Shoot from above and below, and even from inside the parade. Get close enough to show faces, costumes, and details.
5. Shoot while walking. Move along with your subject while things are moving but be prepared to take pictures if the parade comes to a brief stop.

OPPOSITE. *Most parades, like this one in Bali, have too many things going on too quickly. To reduce your frustration, look ahead to see what is coming. Choose a zoom lens with wide-angle capacity so you can get close. Compose to show the line of people, their faces, and costumes, and prefocus—do not use autofocus—on a promising spot. Then shoot as soon as the subject comes into the frame.*

ABOVE. *The excitement and noise of a village parade in Ghana is caught with a telephoto lens using a fast shutter speed.*

On Stage

One of the pleasures of travel is watching performances that are not likely to be found easily at home. Naturally, there is a temptation to bring back mementos of these stagings, especially in foreign countries where souvenir programs may not be sold. Whatever the event—a play, rodeo, circus, street performance, or ritual ceremony—the musicians, dancers, actors, and other performers are often fascinating and colorful photographic subjects.

Yet successful action shots of such performances must be planned. For example, it is best to get a seat that gives you an unobstructed vantage point as close as possible to the stage. If that cannot be done, you may prefer to be at the rear or on a side aisle so you can set up a telephoto lens on a tripod without disturbing other members of the audience.

It is important to develop the ability to anticipate the action. Fortunately, many performances have a rhythm, with actions being repeated. Most likely a dancer will make certain movements in series. At a rodeo or sporting event, contestants will be asked to do the same thing, each in turn. Watch for such patterns and be ready to photograph when they reoccur. In particular, be alert for decisive moments when the action reaches its peak.

With so much going on at once, discipline yourself by being selective. You cannot shoot everything at once, so choose the aspects that you are likely to photograph well. Then take lots of pictures to ensure a few terrific ones.

One of the most difficult aspects to master of performance photography is getting the proper exposure indoors, especially when you want a fairly fast shutter speed to freeze the

By watching carefully and anticipating this Ghanaian dancer's repeated, rhythmic performance, her movement was caught at the peak of action.

action. Remember, your flash unit is not suitable in these situations, and autoexposure cameras often cannot adjust to these lighting conditions. With cameras that feature manual override, it is helpful to meter an area of the stage or arena that has the same brightness as the subject you plan to shoot. For instance, the dirt floor of a rodeo is about the same value as the color of brown horses. When you take the meter reading, avoid bright spots such as lights. Then preset and lock in your exposure, using a shutter speed of at least 1/60 of a second to retain some sharpness.

Autoexposure cameras with electronic flash units will only provide enough light if you are within 20 feet (7 meters) of the subject. Do not waste your time and money shooting with a flash at distances greater than that. One alternative is to use high-speed film indoors—ISO 400 to 800—and bracket using the compensation dial if the background is much brighter or darker than the subject.

If you cannot take the shots you want during a performance, if you would rather relax during the show, or if you want an interesting perspective, try going backstage before and after the performance. Depending on where you are traveling, this may take some determination and diplomacy but often this can be done with few problems. You will be rewarded with a glimpse of the hidden world behind the curtain and a chance to get close to the performers. Here you can use that flash to good effect, going for candid shots, snapshots, and posed shots, depending on your preference and the tolerance of the performers.

Another alternative is to turn your camera around toward the audience. This is a good way to portray local people, as well as your travel companions, enjoying themselves—candids that will add immeasurably to your travel memories.

This colorful dancer saluted us spontaneously right after a Pongal festival performance in Madurai, India. We asked him to repeat his stance for a photograph.

Panning for Action

A specialty technique that photographers employ for shooting on the move is panning. Panning entails following the subject with the camera as it moves across the film plane. The objective is to get the subject reasonably sharp while turning the background into streaks of color or light.

Panning works best with exposures from 1/30 to 1/15 of a second and with multicolored or patterned backgrounds. Lenses in the normal to moderate telephoto (105mm) range enable the photographer to work at a fair distance from the subject, making for a smoother pan.

Try panning at the track to record racing cars or racehorses, for sports such as bicycle riding, boating, skiing, or skating, and for children on carousels or other amusement rides.

To photograph a child riding a horse on a carousel in New York City, the camera was panned at 1/15 of a second, keeping the subject reasonably clear while blurring the lights and the background.

NATURAL MOTIONS

Today's travelers are more and more interested in experiencing nature and glimpsing a vanishing wilderness. Tourism to the national parks and wildlife preserves continues to grow, and photographic safaris are replacing hunting trips, a change we fervently support.

Like hunters, however, photographers must develop an affinity for the wild. For there are patterns to be learned, whether we are stalking wildlife or trying to capture the play of water or wind. We must become familiar with the places where animals or birds live or visit, notice telling tracks and signs, and develop a loving patience and respect for the rhythms of the natural world.

Successful wildlife photography requires knowledge of animal behavior and willingness to adjust your itinerary accordingly. Obviously, it is not possible to make appointments with wildlife to suit your schedule. And if you arrive at the wrong time, you will be disappointed, no matter how many animals or birds are actually out there. In general, animals feed at the extremes of the day, when they can be found at their favorite watering spots, grazing grounds, rookeries, and nesting areas.

Professional wildlife photographers know the habits of their subjects. They often shoot at close range by setting up blinds and using electronic-eye triggering devices that fire the shutter at exactly the right moment. High-quality nature photography takes an enormous amount of time, often with weeks and months elapsing before capturing the exciting action shots you see in nature magazines and films.

Since wildlife photography is so dependent on being familiar with a species, its behavior, and its habitat, many travelers prefer going "on safari" with professionals who know the local terrain intimately. While these trips increase the odds of finding animals, keep in mind that they may not be engaged

The sea's rhythmic movement is captured at the instant a wave crashes on the shore of Maine's Acadia National Park.

in exciting action when you find them. They will probably be resting, grazing, drinking, or caring for their young. Still, just sighting wildlife is exhilarating to most of us. And if you shoot typical animal behaviors—yawning, scratching, feeding, take-offs, and landings—you will be proud of your portfolio.

But there is more to natural motion than wildlife. In fact, the movement of water and wind can yield some very evocative photographs, whether in the wild or in more civilized settings. And there is room for experimentation, as these elements occur no matter where your travels take you.

Birds on the Wing

Photographing birds is one of the most demanding—and satisfying—obsessions. More than with other wildlife, the photographer must get close, even with a telephoto lens, so the image of the bird will fill the frame, or at least be recognizable.

Fortunately, birds are creatures of habit, which is advantageous, provided we know their habits and are willing to adapt to them. Our likelihood of getting successful photographs increases if we look for birds in environments that make them accessible: in coastal areas; in wetlands, marshes, and bogs; perched on posts, lines, piers, and pilings; in nesting areas and rookeries; behind boats; or at feeders. The many birds that inhabit woodlands are difficult to find and even harder to photograph, unless you are prepared to devote a great deal of time and effort.

Birds' habits point the photographer toward likely actions to shoot. By watching birds as they take off and land, especially in rookeries and nesting areas, as they perform grooming behaviors, or as they stalk their prey, we can begin to anticipate their moves. Think ahead, preset your exposure and focus, then wait for the bird to repeat the pattern.

Because birds are usually photographed at some distance, special equipment is needed. Ideally, use a fast telephoto lens—a 400mm, f/2.8 lens is best, but at a cost of several thousand dollars, it is prohibitive for most nonprofessionals. A more affordable alternative is a 400mm, f/5.6 lens. A powerful telephoto lens should be set on a tripod to provide stability and prevent camera shake.

To catch those flits, flickers, and elusive moments, use a fast film (ISO 200 to 1000) and a camera with a built-in winder, as well as the fastest possible shutter speed.

Animals in the Wild

There is nothing quite as exciting as seeing and photographing animals in the wild. To get a decent picture, the photographer has to be close enough to create a recognizable image. This requires a telephoto lens of at least 200mm.

Some animals have adapted to a human presence or are not so skittish if we get close. Bighorn sheep, deer, and small herds of buffalo can be found in many national parks in open areas that make it possible to get as close as 15 feet (5 meters) from the animals, an adequate distance for portraits if you use a lens in the 35mm to 100mm range. At this distance, by adding light so a smaller f-stop can be used, an electronic flash will add sparkle to the animal's eye, stop movement, and sharpen the image.

At distances too far for a flash to reach, use a spot meter or center weighted meter to get an accurate reading for exposure on the animal, especially if the background is considerably darker or brighter than your subject, such as a buffalo in the snow.

If getting close is out of the question, aim for environmental shots that show the relationship of the animal to the setting. Such photographs may not qualify for a nature magazine, but they will certainly reveal your experience and evoke the mood of the natural environment. To help stabilize a long lens when shooting at such great distances, set your camera on a tripod or rest it on a beanbag placed on a rock, car roof, or other support.

For action shots, show a typical behavior of the animal by taking a sequence of pictures with a fast shutter speed. You may need to take many photographs to ensure getting a few good ones that capture the most telling moments. For example, bighorn sheep typically graze at Yellowstone National Park by moving up the slope gradually. The progression of photographs made by shooting as they inch their way up will likely yield a few that represent the best combination of action, composition, and light.

Faster kinds of motion, such as a fox scampering across a field, record well using a panning technique. This involves following the animals with the camera hand-held while the aperture is open, at shutter speeds of 1/60 to 1/15 of a second. The image may not be crystal clear, but if done well, it will capture the essence of the animal's movement. Fast films (ISO 200 to 1000) help freeze motion by making it possible to combine fast shutter speeds with small aperture settings.

Portraits of wild animals require a powerful telephoto lens and a willingness to move in quite close. This longhorn sheep was grazing along a mountainside in Yellowstone National Park in Wyoming during winter.

At the Zoo

Photographing animals in zoos can become an end in itself, as well as a productive way to learn and practice for photography in the wild. A clear advantage of photographing zoo animals is that you know they will be there, and will be reasonably close. With effort, you can produce animal portraits that would be nearly impossible elsewhere.

As with wildlife photography, it is important to visit the animals at the right time, whether that means in the spring or early summer, when babies are born; at feeding times; or just when the weather is sufficiently moderate to encourage lively activity. And be sure to look in all directions, not just straight ahead: you may find a lion sleeping in a tree or an aquatic creature, such as an otter, down in the water.

Consider your subject's background and incorporate it if the setting simulates the natural environment. What could be more appropriate to show, for example, than a koala in a tree. If the background contains distractions, however, such as people, snack bars, or garbage cans, either camouflage the distraction imaginatively or do not take the picture. An interesting alternative is to use dark shadows in the background to create a stark, studiolike backdrop. You may need to underexpose to deepen the shadows and set off your subject.

In zoos with bars and wire cages, use a wide open aperture to blur out the foreground. Place your camera right up against the cage, focus on the animal in the distance, then look through the lens. The wires should vanish by virtue of selective focus and your use of a narrow depth of field.

TOP. *Spring is the time to find zoo animals interacting with their newborn. For this monochromatic picture of a polar bear nursing her cub in an open enclosure, the ground was metered and a fast shutter speed was used.*

RIGHT. *At zoos, photographers can get close and fill a frame with an animal's image without needing telephoto lenses. This peacock displayed his striking tail feathers while strutting on a walkway at the Barbados Zoo.*

Shooting the Breeze

The movement of the wind is often considered a nuisance when we want to take photographs. But there are times when a breeze can actually create a striking image.

While wandering around the island of Gorée in Senegal—a touch of the Mediterranean in West Africa—we noticed a curtain gently blowing through a window. The combination of weathered pastel paint on the building, the bright blue shutter, and the sheer white curtain was sufficiently interesting in its own right. But then we saw a spot of red deep in the interior—probably late afternoon sunlight striking a painted door—that was visible for a fraction of a second as the curtain ballooned out. The photograph was taken after watching several repetitions of the curtain flapping, then timing the shutter release just before the critical instant, using a fast shutter speed of 1/125 of a second to freeze the curtain's motion.

The wind's effect can also be captured with a slow shutter speed. On a visit to Colorado's Great Sand Dunes National Monument, we were working on a science-oriented assignment on how sand dunes form and migrate. We hoped to produce an image that displayed how wind propels sand from one side of the dune to the other. Fortunately we located a spot where a dark shadow provided a backdrop for the trajectory of sidelit sand. The photograph—shot at a slow shutter speed of 1/2 of a second—graphically documents this natural phenomenon.

Impressionistic as well as documentary photographs can be produced by recording windblown objects with a slow shutter speed. Flowers and grasses, so difficult to capture outdoors just because they are often tossed by the breeze, can be transformed into enchanting blurs of color and shape.

A very fast shutter speed stopped the swaying of palm fronds as a strong wind whipped the coastline of the low-lying Maldives. The low perspective and vertical format of the composition places the sun-drenched palm tree against a polarized sky.

Moving Water

Most photographers want to record the impression of running water, whether in waterfalls, cascades, streams, or fountains. Photographing the movement of water is most easily accomplished by using a slow shutter speed—1/15 to 1/2 of a second—which turns the water into a soft, milky stream. For such long exposures, set your camera on a tripod or another sturdy support.

Such time exposure techniques work best in conditions of low, uniform light, such as in shade or on overcast days. Uniform light not only avoids any bright highlights, which would compete with and distract from the water, but it also simplifies getting a proper exposure and enhances the velvety quality of the moving water.

On a recent trip through Idaho, we came upon water sprinklers irrigating huge fields, beautifully backlit. The pattern of the sprays captured our imaginations, and we experimented with timing and shutter speeds to find the right combination to convey the shape of the competing arcs of water, as well as the misty pulsing of the spouts. The results we liked best, out of twenty frames taken, turned out to be shot at 1/125 of a second, enough to give definition to the precise moment when the spurt or water shot out.

Another way to use the motion of water occurred to us as we watched gondolas bobbing in Venice. A slow shutter speed of 1/4 of a second produced the image we liked best. But the exact degree of blurring that appeals to the photographer is a matter of personal aesthetic preference.

TOP. *An eruption of the world-famous geyser, Old Faithful, is photographed against the backlight of sunrise in Wyoming's Yellowstone National Park. The underexposure of the sky accentuates the contrast between the steaming water vapor and the sky.*

RIGHT. *The milky effect of moving water is accomplished by shooting at a slow shutter speed under uniform, low-contrast light conditions. This cascade in Montana's Glacier National Park was taken after metering the rocks and underexposing half a stop.*

9
A Change of
Pace

"First comes the discovery. Then
follows the work. And sometimes
something from it remains."

IN A DIFFERENT LIGHT

This chapter is for those eager to expand their photographic repertoire as traveling photographers by learning how to work with artificial light and by experimenting with special effects. We have already discussed (in chapter 3) the potential of natural light at various times of the day and in different kinds of weather. Here we explore the possibilities of working with artificial light sources, from electronic flash and candlelight to floodlight. This type of photography is often overlooked, or misunderstood, by many traveling shutterbugs. Amateur photographers either avoid taking such pictures altogether, thinking artificial light is impossible or difficult to manage, or they use faulty techniques that produce disappointing images.

In the natural world we often encounter a mix of different light sources all at once. We may want to combine a rosy sky at dusk with streetlights or to break the rules by shooting incandescent light with daylight film. Understanding how artificial light affects film will enhance your photographic options. A little technical know-how will enable you to notice new visual opportunities, and will help you develop a more personal photographic style.

This chapter will reveal a few tricks and gimmicks in image-making—some interesting ways to manipulate your equipment and some after-the-fact twists to give your photographs pizazz. Yet these techniques are not difficult. And if you are looking for a push in an exciting direction, they will take you beyond the scope of usual travel photographs.

PAGES 208–209. *For an interesting change of pace, two images—one of the coastline of Mykonos, the other of a sunset—were overlapped to produce this "sandwich."*

ABOVE. *To counterbalance the bright daylight on the background Samurai wall in Hagi, Japan, low-power, fill-in flash was added to illuminate this streetcleaner's face.*

Electronic Flash

Today's flash units are small, smart, and handy sources of ready-to-use artificial light. Many cameras have built-in flash units that save space and effort. Removable flash units with heads that rotate and tilt are more versatile but can only be mounted on cameras with hotshoes.

No matter where you go, flash units can provide the light to create professional-looking photographs. But to make the most of these sophisticated electronic devices, understand what they can and cannot do. In fact, they do more than most of us think by illuminating people and scenes with tailor-made light output and with split-second timing. What they cannot do—and too many amateur forget this—is light up large expanses, like the Grand Canyon or the Roman Colosseum.

Here are some ways to use your flash unit:

1. Fill-in flash. This burst of light that is less powerful than the full flash eliminates or softens shadows in high-contrast light, such as bright daylight. For example, a hat brim may cast a dark shadow over a person's face. Fill-in flash adds just enough light to illuminate the shadow portion, without overpowering the surrounding daylight. The desired effect is to match the intensity of the daylight, so the flash becomes invisible. Fill-in flash can also brighten colors made dull by being in shade or in dim light.
2. Freeze action. The burst of light provided by an electronic flash unit can stop motion in daylight and at night. The speed of the flash—usually greater than 1/750 second—rather than the shutter speed, determines the true length of exposure. Try using your flash unit if you want a sharp, crisp shot of a child in perpetual motion.
3. Rear curtain flash. An interesting new variation on stopping motion exists in state-of-the-art SLR cameras with rear curtain or second curtain flash capability. This automatic system combines flash with a long exposure. The shutter remains open for as long as needed—1/8 of a second or longer—to expose the ambient light of the scene. The flash fires an instant before the shutter closes, illuminating the moving subject. This combination produces a natural looking scene with a ghostlike blur trailing behind the subject.

This effect can be approximated in SLRs with manual override by setting the shutter speed at a level slower than the synchronization speed recommended for the flash unit. At 1/2 to 1/15 of a second, a ghost effect can be created in this manner.

Before you travel test your flash unit to make sure it works properly and to check its power output.

Full-power electronic flash was needed for proper exposure on the face of this woman at a ceremonial "sing-sing" in Papua, New Guinea.

Incandescent Light

Traveling photographers will find incandescent light not only in many indoor light bulbs, but also in outdoor floodlights, car headlights, candles, and some streetlamps. Indoor scenes lit with incandescent bulbs sparkle with unusual color. And monumental architecture appears more splendid at night when bathed with floodlights.

Because incandescent light has a warmer color than white daylight, photographs taken in this light using daylight film have a yellow-orange cast. Ordinarily, photographers are advised to neutralize this color shift. This can be done by using film especially balanced for incandescent light, called tungsten film, or by using an 80A or 80B conversion filter. But the effects of incandescent light with daylight film are often pleasing to the eye. An 81C conversion filter adds to the warm, evocative glow or romantic mood.

Even a single candle can provide enough light to illuminate a room and the people in it, thanks to the way film accumulates light. The wedding scene we photographed in a dark church in Odessa is a case in point. Knowing that the church's interior would be dark, we had brought along a flash unit and very fast film of ISO 3200. Once inside, we realized that the mood of the wedding and the rosy glow of the scene could only be retained if the photograph was taken by the light of the candle held by the bride. A shutter speed of 1/60 of a second minimized the effects of movement, and the graininess of the fast film enhanced the special mood of the occasion.

Here are a few pointers for making the most of incandescent light:

1. Do not meter bright areas. This will distort exposure, leaving much of the scene dark. Instead, spot meter or take a close-up reading of a middle-tone shadow area, or the most important subject or color in the frame. Then lock in that reading before composing and shooting.
2. Do not activate your flash. To retain the warm glow of incandescent light, make that your only or chief light source. A flash will dominate and overwhelm the softer incandescent light.
3. Keep the camera steady. Brace yourself or use a tripod for camera stability during the longer exposures usually needed with incandescent light.

The orange color of pumpkins in a New Hampshire barn is enhanced by the incandescent (tungsten) light taken with film balanced for daylight.

Mixed Light

Traveling photographers can create strange and eerie colors by mixing varied light sources on film. The way colors appear depends to some extent on the type of film selected. Films balanced for one kind of light—for example, daylight or incandescent light—will register colors in dramatically different ways if shot in any other light. When several light sources occur together, as they do at dusk or at night, even ordinary scenes can take on an ethereal look.

A street scene shot at night with daylight film, for example, will render incandescent light as yellow-orange and mercury vapor light as green. On the other hand, tungsten film will turn the night sky a deep royal blue, producing a truly psychedelic look, while the lights of a building remain white.

To make the most of these interesting possibilities, consider the following:

1. Shoot with daylight film around sunset to combine ambient light with artificial light. The warm tones of dusk or the rich blues just afterward work well with the light of street lamps, moving headlights and taillights, boat lights, and floodlights.
2. Shoot with tungsten film at sunset to alter the colors dramatically toward blue and magenta.
3. Long exposure times—from 5 seconds to 1 minute—will be needed to create streaks of color from moving lights. Use a slow film—ISO 25 to 64—for such long exposures. Since these situations are so variable, take many photos at different exposure times to experiment.
4. Use a flash with low ambient light (slow down shutter speed) for capturing the atmosphere of a location by incorporating a brightly lit foreground object.

A fiery sunset light sets off the glow of a streetlamp to provide color interest for this sculptural silhouette taken in New York City's Battery Park.

Special Effects

While photographic images rely on visual realities for their raw material, they can be manipulated and transformed in intriguing ways. These special effects make it possible to rescue less than ideal pictures or to create more exciting or dramatic images than those seen by the eye or the camera.

One such effect involves zooming a lens during exposure, which is an interesting alternative to straight documentary photography. In the resulting image, action is exaggerated or the excitement of movement is created, even where none exists. Bright lights against a dark nighttime sky are especially suitable for zooming.

This technique requires a zoom lens; an 80mm to 200mm zoom is recommended for the maximum zoom effect. The zoomed image is made by moving the barrel of the lens in or out during a long exposure. A brief pause at the start or end of the zoom freezes the image of the main subject. The technique is simple:

1. Place the camera on a tripod.
2. Focus on a central subject, such as a skyscraper, with the zoom lens at its most telephoto.
3. Use a small aperture—f/8 or smaller—to maximize sharpness.
4. Meter the central subject with a spot meter and choose a shutter speed of 1/15 of a second or longer.

TOP. *Zooming is a special effect that works especially well at night when long exposures are necessary. This zoom shot of the New York City skyline was taken from New Jersey's Liberty State Park.*

LEFT. *Two overexposed, dissimilar, and uninspired images of Venice—a blue barge and a typical canal scene—are salvaged by combining, or sandwiching, them into a striking picture. In this way, accidentally overexposed photos can be rescued with this special effect.*

5. Zoom the lens during the long exposure, moving it toward its widest range.

The specific effect will vary depending on how smoothly or erratically the zooming is done. Experiment with exposure times and zooming motions. For example, try moving the barrel of the lens toward or away from your body to determine which motion is more comfortable.

Another interesting effect is called sandwiching. True to its name, sandwiching involves overlapping two or more images to create a new single image. That bland sky can be replaced by a brilliant sunset or a puffy cloud. Various aspects of the same location can be merged into a single montage. Sandwiching is also a way to salvage otherwise unsatisfactory images through imaginative recycling.

Sandwiched images can be prepared after the fact, by trial and error, or by experimentation. With transparencies, these combined images can be seen easily on a lightbox; envisioning the results with negatives is somewhat more difficult.

Experienced travel photographers, however, plan for some sandwiches during their travels. We recommend taking several overexposures at 1/2 stop increments and with the subject at different parts of the frame to give yourself greatest flexibility in matching with other images.

With automatic cameras, set the compensation dial to +1/2 and +1 for the same degree of overexposure.

TOP. *The dull sky in this Dutch landscape was improved after the fact by adding a stronger image of a darker, cloudy sky. The net effect is a more dramatic sky and richer colors in the tulip field of the original image.*

RIGHT. *A sandwich can be deliberately planned and composed from separate images. These Dutch windmills were shot against a stark evening sky with the idea that an image of the moon would be superimposed on it. Room was left for adding the moon on the upper right.*

10
Great Travel
Photographs

*". . . I want to take pictures of
everything and send them to my
friends."*

JOHN WESLEY POWELL, 1865

In contrast to our age of visual bombardment and instantaneous satellite transmission, it is hard to imagine that only 150 years ago, few people knew what the world looked like beyond their immediate surroundings. And still fewer individuals had seen distant lands with their own eyes. Those who did travel, from necessity or a spirit of adventure, faced extraordinary hardships and uncertainties, but the reward was a sense of personal discovery.

Through revolutions in transportation and communication, including photography, the world seemed smaller, more accessible, and considerably more familiar. Many of the earliest photographic images were made during travels undertaken for scientific or purely commercial purposes.

We owe these photographic pioneers a real debt, for travel pictures influenced us all in so many ways. Not only did they introduce us to the wonders of faraway places, they also inspired people to explore the world themselves. There were other benefits as well. In making us aware of the natural beauty of the American West, for example, vast tracts of unspoiled wilderness came to be protected as national parks for future generations. Photographs also revealed the marvels of art and architecture, including long neglected ancient ruins that came to be treasured, preserved, and restored. And these travel images reminded us both of the diversity and similarity of peoples, countering an inclination toward insularity.

The early photographers overcame frustration as they transported all the tools needed to ply their trade, often hauling their heavy loads over inhospitable terrain. Cameras in those days were huge, and pictures were made on glass plates, not film. Each picture had to be processed individually on the spot. As a result, photographers had to lug a portable darkroom and plenty of chemicals. Amazingly, the resulting photographs were often not just serviceable documents but works that have become part of our visual heritage.

In selecting a sampling of important photographs for this chapter, we imposed limitations. First, we chose only works of photographers who traveled far from home. Great photogra-

FRANCIS FRITH, "PYRAMIDS FROM THE SOUTHWEST, GIZA," 1858. *Frith took up photography in England around 1850 after a decade working as a grocer. During three expeditions to the Middle East, his photographs were numerous enough to fill nine volumes, including the largest photographs then published in books. With its simple, elegant composition, this early photograph, 15 x 19 1/4 in. (38 x 48.8 cm), taken in Egypt, sets the stage for future images of the pyramid.*

PAGE 216. WILLIAM ANDERS, "EARTHRISE," 1969. *A portent of things to come, this remarkable image of Earth was taken from the moon by amateur photographer Anders, an astronaut aboard Apollo 8. Not unlike other voyagers, Anders was drawn to the unexpected: "Our Earth was quite colorful, pretty, and delicate compared to the very rough, rugged, beat-up, even boring lunar surface. We'd come 240,000 miles to see the moon, and it was the Earth that was really worth looking at."*

phers like Eugène Atget and Josef Sudek, whose cameras captured stirring images of Paris and Prague, were, therefore, not considered. Also, we favored those who were among the first to venture into particular regions—people like Francis Frith in Egypt and Carleton E. Watkins in the American West—and who awakened public interest with their fascinating depictions. Finally, we wanted to present several recent photographers who brought an individual vision and technique to travel subjects.

ABOVE. CARLETON E. WATKINS, "THE VALLEY FROM MARIPOSA TRAIL, YOSEMITE, CALIFORNIA," C. 1863. *Though born in Oneonta, New York, Watkins settled in California in 1850 and made his reputation photographing the American West. He photographed Yosemite, starting in 1861, and returned there five years later as the official photographer for the U.S. Geological Survey.*

ABOVE RIGHT. WILLIAM HENRY JACKSON, "OLD FAITHFUL GEYSER, YELLOWSTONE PARK," C. 1870. *After the Civil War, Jackson, a veteran, moved from Troy, New York to Omaha, Nebraska in 1858. His photographic work for the U.S. Geological Survey from 1870 to 1878 documenting the Rocky Mountains landscape was instrumental in establishing the first national park at Yellowstone. Here is one of Jackson's most famous portrayals of Old Faithful.*

OPPOSITE, TOP LEFT. GEORGE SHIRAS III, "SANDY LAKE, NEWFOUNDLAND," 1908. *A lawyer, biologist, and congressman, who sponsored legislation to protect wildlife in the early years of this century, Shiras also took up photography. In fact he invented new methods of night photography and became a "hunter" of scenics. This image sets a mood of a peace and tranquility while revealing Shiras' technical skill.*

OPPOSITE, BOTTOM LEFT. JOHN DUDLEY JOHNSTON, "LIVERPOOL—AN IMPRESSION," 1906. *Johnston's work shows the influence of the "Links," a group of English amateur photographers whose new aesthetic attitudes promoted an impressionistic treatment of all subject matter. Here, the shapes and tonalities of a Liverpool cityscape are rendered through an atmospheric haze created by a special printing process.*

ABOVE. ADAM CLARK VROMAN, "HOPI MAIDEN,"
C. 1902. *Leaving his native Illinois to settle in
California after his wife died in 1895, Vroman
began documenting the life of the Hopi and other
Southwestern Indians. His interest was more ethno-
logical than aesthetic, and he portrayed the people
and their activities with simplicity and dignity.
Vroman was so modest about his abilities that he
was surprised his work drew attention at an exhibition in 1900 at the California Camera Club.*

BELOW. JAKE RAJS, "THE SIERRA NEVADA, CALIFORNIA," 1981. *Born in Poland, Rajs came to the United States as a child. After a false start in engineering, he turned his artistic talents to writing, painting, and sculpture. Finally settling on a career in commercial and travel photography, Rajs has worked in countries around the world. This landscape photograph is a good example of his elegant use of color, line, and light.*

BOTTOM. SAM ABELL, "RED SQUARE SEEN FROM A HOTEL WINDOW," 1983. *An American contract photographer for the National Geographic since he was twenty-six years old, Abell has been assigned to cover stories around the world. His images exquisitely balance photojournalism and art. Here, Abell fuses the disparate elements of a lace curtain, pears on a window sill, and the Kremlin's architecture into an imaginative composition of light and form.*

ABOVE. BRIAN BRAKE, "BUDDHIST TEMPLE OF SANZEN-IN, KYOTO," 1964. *A native of New Zealand, Brake traveled extensively in the Far East, photographing for publications and exhibitions. His two favorite destinations were Japan and China, where he was one of the first outsiders to take photographs after China's revolution in 1949. He considers this image one that depicts the essence of Japan.*

APPENDIX
AFTER THE TRIP

SHARING MEMORIES

The moment when we open our packets of processed film is always frought with a mix of excitement and anxiety. We are eager to see the results of our photographic endeavors, but we secretly worry if our equipment and our imaginations were in fine working order. Will the pictures recreate the spirit of the trip as we experienced it? Will they recall moments and sights we may have forgotten? Will they convey to others what we saw and felt? Will they be technically proficient? Interesting? Original?

All these thoughts flood through our minds as we begin to inspect the slides or prints we have taken. Our first concerns tend to be technical, because without proper exposure and sharpness we will have little to show. We may decide to keep some less than perfect specimens if they represent the best option for a hard-to-get subject or difficult situation. For example, snapshots taken of people's momentary expressions or during a one-time event may not be ideal, but they may be worth keeping and showing for personal rather than pictorial reasons. Such photographs tend to improve with age, if only because they recall fond memories that might otherwise be lost.

Next, we begin the difficult process of editing the photographs. This is hard in two ways. First, we feel a certain attachment to all the pictures. They are our creations, our progeny, and we love them all equally, whether or not they deserve it. Also, while we try to be objective, our decisions are inevitably colored by the feelings we had at the time the pictures were taken. We tend to overlook flaws that may be obvious to viewers who were not there with us.

If the photographs are only for our own amusement, we can indulge our indiscriminate loyalty to any images we choose. However, if we intend to share our work with others—either informally in albums and slide shows or more formally through publication or public display—then we need to exercise far greater selectivity and organization.

This is so not just because outsiders will be less forgiving of our flaws—in fact, their standards may be lower than ours. It is primarily because sharing what we do with others requires greater coherence and purpose. If we are to communicate our ideas, experiences and feelings to those who were not there, we must take into account the observer's interests and capacity to appreciate what we have done. We must structure our experience in ways that will have meaning for those who did not share it, inviting them to partake and imaginatively relive it with us.

Editing and presenting—the subjects of this chapter—are the often-neglected skills in photography instruction which can make the difference between effective and ineffective photographic displays. Too often the impression is left that all excellence in photography is achieved in the camera. Leaving aside the roles of processing, printing and reproduction in the creation of quality, a great deal is achieved, or can be, during the selection and organization stages of any photographic presentation.

When done with clarity and flair, the whole should be larger than the sum of its parts. The value of individual photographs is enhanced as they are orchestrated into a new visual totality.

SELECTING WHAT TO SHOW

The selection and editing process is crucial to the effectiveness of your photo presentation. You must develop an uncharacteristic ruthlessness as you review your travel photographs, eliminating from consideration any pictures that serve no clear purpose for you. Here's what that means:

1. Don't repeat yourself. If you have several variations of the same shot, decide which is the best, and use that one alone. Send spares to family or friends.
2. Always consider technical value. Few people are interested

in looking at severely under- or over-exposed pictures. Eliminate them except in the most dire circumstances.

3. Keep in mind your editorial purpose. Each picture should tell a little story or reveal an interesting point about your trip. The more each photograph tells, the richer it is in editorial content, and the better your presentation will be.

4. Emphasize your personal touch. Include photographs that show your imagination, originality and creativity at work, or that demonstrate your personal perspective on the sights and people you encountered during your journey.

5. Think thematically. Try to bring into focus a few main points about your trip. Build your selections around those themes to develop groupings within your presentation. For example, if your interest is folk culture, show the aspects of a particular culture in a reasonably systematic way. Or if you're fascinated by architecture, explore that theme explicitly.

6. Show variety. If you find that your pictures all look alike, expand your repetoire so your travel photographs will reflect the diversity of all you saw.

7. Tell a story. Think of your presentation as a visual story-telling, with a beginning, middle and end. It could follow the course of your trip, chronologically. Or it can combine chronology with thematic elements. The important thing is don't feel that you must show your photographs in the order in which they were taken. Like a movie maker, you can shoot in one sequence, but show in another.

PREPARING PRESENTATIONS

Once your selections are made, you are ready to arrange them in a way that will convey visual and editorial coherence. Much will depend on the nature and purpose of your travels. A trip to the Grand Canyon would not be well-represented by a long series of close-up portraits of your travel companions, even if their faces were interesting and you became the best of friends.

If you have edited carefully, your task now is to decide on how best to organize your final selections. The order and sequence of photographs, in an album or on a screen, has visual meaning. And since looking at pictures is a visual experience, you should keep in mind the impact the photographs will make, as they are viewed next to each other on a page or one after another on a screen. At the same time, you will want to recreate the flow of your journey and display your photographic interests and skills.

That's a tall order, but one worth trying to fill. Here are some specific suggestions to make it easier:

1. Design a strong layout. Old-fashioned albums allow for prints of different sizes and formats on a page, and have room for caption-writing. (These also avoid the plastic sleeves that often destroy prints over time.) Choose the prints you want together in a single or double-page spread. Lay out the prints and move them around until they create an appealing arrangement. Look at books and magazine layouts to get ideas and inspiration. Secure the prints once you are satisfied. Prepare captions which identify locations and people on separate labels, to be affixed afterward.

2. Keep it short. Slide presentations should not exceed one hour, if possible. If your presentation is much longer, invite your audience back for part two. This means that your slide presentation should fit into one tray of 80 or 140 slides. Knowing your limits, you can restrict your slide selection to that number and concentrate on showing only your best work.

3. Create a visual and narrative sequence. Lay out slides on a light box, first in thematic groups. Then draw from these groups to fill a chronological order. Finally, rearrange the sequence to provide for the best juxtapositions of narrative and visual elements. Tell your story, but stay aware of the impact of one image following another. For example, you may have a general market scene followed by a close-up of a vendor. If the colors and composition of the two images seem repetitive or incompatible, select a different vendor's face from your thematic group. Shift and reorganize the sequence on the lightbox until you are satisfied. Then project the entire show in advance and fine tune it as you watch.

4. Jazz it up. For a more ambitious presentation, try adding title slides, synchronizing with music on an audiotape, or using a dual-projector system.

FILL-IN FLASH

For eliminating or softening shadows, an electronic flash unit is a versatile accessory for the outdoor photographer. The flash unit may be set to provide just enough fill-in light to give detail to the shaded areas without eliminating shadows, or the flash may be set to avoid shadows entirely. Fill-in flash is best used between 3 and 15 feet from the subject.

There are so many camera and flash systems on the market that it is not possible to give specific instructions for each. However, the principles and steps listed below provide a general guide to the effective use of fill-in flash.

For flash units with variable power ratios:

1. Set flash unit to proper ISO designation, for example, 100.
2. Set camera shutter speed to designated flash synchronization speed. Most cameras synchronize at 1/60 of a second or slower.
3. Carefully meter the highlights, that is, the brightest parts of the subject, with the camera's shutter speed set at the synchronization speed for flash photography.
4. Focus on the subject to determine the flash-to-subject distance. This distance is found on the focusing scale of the lens barrel.
5. To determine flash output for this distance, set the flash unit for manual operation. Turn the dial on the flash unit so the flash-to-subject distance and the highlight meter reading are aligned. An arrow or indicator will point to the suggested power level.
6. This power level should be reduced by 1 f-stop for purposes of fill-in flash. Therefore, use the next lower power level from the one suggested. For example, if the meter reading is f/11 and the flash-to-subject distance is 9 feet, the recommended power level may be 1/2 of power. For fill-in flash, set the flash unit at 1/4 of power.
7. Take the photograph. Bracket by changing the f-stop at 1/2-stop intervals.

For flash units with constant power output:

1. Set flash unit to proper ISO designation, for example, 100.
2. Set camera shutter speed to designated flash synchronization speed. Most cameras synchronize at 1/60 of a second or slower.
3. Carefully meter the highlights, that is, the brightest parts of the subject, with the camera's shutter speed set at the synchronization speed for flash photography.
4. Focus on the subject to determine the flash-to-subject distance. This distance is found on the focusing scale of the lens barrel.
5. The dial on the flash unit will recommend a particular f-stop at this flash-to-subject distance. Compare the recommended f-stop to the meter reading..
6. If the meter reading and recommended f-stop are the same (e.g., 1/60 of a second at f/8), or if the meter reading calls for a higher f-stop than the one suggested on the flash unit dial (e.g., a meter reading of 1/60 of a second at f/16 and a recommended f-stop of f/8), then the power output of the flash unit can be reduced in one of two ways:
   a. by covering the flash unit with layers of lens tissue to achieve the desired reduction of light output.
   b. or by removing the flash unit from the camera and placing it at a greater distance from the subject.
7. If the meter reading calls for an f-stop that is 1 stop lower than the one recommended on the flash unit (e.g., the meter reading is 1/60 of a second at f/11 and the recommended f-stop is f/16), then no compensation is needed, and the photograph can be taken.
8. If the meter reading calls for an f-stop that is 2 or more stops lower than the one recommended on the flash unit (e.g., the meter reading is 1/60 of a second at f/11 and the recommended f-stop is f/22), then move the flash closer to the subject.
9. Another way to reduce power with fill-in flash is to increase the ISO number on the flash unit or on your camera if it con-

trols the flash output. This change fools the built-in computerized electronic mechanism into producing less illumination based on the assumption that a faster film is being used. Doubling the ISO number is equivalent to a reduction of 1 full f-stop. Intermediate reductions can be made proportionately.

10. It is also possible to reduce light output by covering the flash head with two sheets of lens tissue. The loss of light will be approximately 1 f-stop. The resulting image will show little change in the background lighting, but the shadows in the foreground will be brightened.

COLOR CORRECTION CHART

The chart below shows how to remove a color cast from a photographic subject so, the light records on the film as if it were a white, colorless light. The first column indicates the type of film in the camera. To use this chart, find the description of light that matches the available conditions, outdoors or indoors, and check the colors of light that may prevail. Moving horizontally across the chart, locate the suggested color correction filter, and adjust the exposure by the amount listed in the last column. For example, using daylight film at a high mountain elevation on a clear day, the light may have a bluish cast. Correct this with an 81A or 81B filter, and overexpose by 1/2 of an f-stop.

Film	Description of Light	Color of Light	Suggested Filter	Exposure Correction
Daylight	Sunrise/sunset	Magenta	82C	+1/2
		Bluish	81A or 81B	+1/2
		Yellow	82A	+1/3
Daylight	Overcast	Bluish gray	81A or 81B	+1/2
Daylight	High mountain, clear	Blue	81A or 81B	+1/2
	High mountain, hazy	Bluish gray	1B	None

Film	Description of Light	Color of Light	Suggested Filter	Exposure Correction
Daylight	Midday sunlight	Slightly blue	1A or 1B	None
Daylight	Shade	Blue	81 series	+1/3
Daylight	Fluorescent	Greenish	FL-D	None
Tungsten	Fluorescent	Bluish	FL-B	None
Daylight	Tungsten (type B)	Yellowish	80A	+2
Daylight	Tungsten (type A)	Yellowish	80B	+1 1/2

TECHNICAL INFORMATION

Numbers in **bold type** refer to page numbers.
An asterisk indicates that this picture was taken with a "point-and-shoot" camera.

Jacket, front: Fujichrome 50, f/22 at 1/30 second, tripod.
Jacket, back: Fujichrome 50, f/8 with flash.
1: Fujichrome 100, 35mm lens.*
2–3: Kodachrome 64, 35–200mm zoom lens, 1/125 second, f/5.6.
8–9: Fujichrome 100, 35mm lens, f/11 at 1/250 second.

12: Kodachrome 64, 100mm lens, f/8.
13: Fujichrome Velvia, f/11 at 1/8 second, tripod.
14, left: Kodachrome 64, f/5.6 at 1/250 second.
14, right: Kodachrome 64, 35–70mm zoom lens, f/5.6.
15, opposite: Kodachrome 64, 24mm

lens, f/8 at 1/250 second.
16–17: Kodachrome 64, 180mm lens, f/8 at 1/125 second.
18: Fujichrome 50, 50–250mm zoom lens, f/16 at 1/8 second, tripod.
19: Fujichrome 100, 50–250mm zoom lens at 250mm, f/16 at 1/8 second.
20: Fujichrome 100, 35–70mm zoom lens

at 50mm, f/8.
21: Kodachrome 64, 24mm lens, f/5.6.
22: Fujichrome 100, 35–70mm zoom lens at 70mm, f/5.6, tripod.
23, top: Kodachrome 64, 35–70mm zoom lens at 35mm.*
23, bottom: Kodachrome 64, 35mm lens, f/5.6.

24, **right**: Ektachrome 64, 50mm macro lens fills the frame with detail, f/8 at 1/4 second, tripod.

25, **top**: Kodachrome 25, 35mm lens, f/16, tripod.

25, **bottom**: Kodachrome 64, 28mm lens, f/8 at 1/15 second.

26: Fujichrome 50, 35–70mm zoom lens at 35mm, f/16, tripod.

27: Fujichrome 100, 35–70mm zoom lens at 35mm.*

28, **top**: Fujichrome 100, 35–70mm zoom lens, f/16, tripod.

28, **bottom**: Kodachrome 64, 28mm lens, f/11, tripod

29, **top**: Kodachrome 64, 50mm lens, f/16 at 1/30 second, tripod.

29, **bottom**: Fujichrome Velvia, 50–250mm zoom lens at 180mm, f/8 at 1/15 second, tripod.

30, **top**: Fujichrome 100, 35–70mm zoom lens at 70mm, f/11.

30, **bottom**: Kodachrome 64, 35mm lens, f/8.

31: Fujichrome 50, 35–70mm zoom lens at 70mm, f/5.6 at 1/30 second, tripod.

32, **left**: Fujichrome 100, 50–250mm zoom lens at 200mm, f/5.6.

32, **right**: Kodachrome 64, 35mm lens, f/5.6 at 1/60 second.

33: Fujichrome 100, 35mm lens.*

34: Fujichrome 100, 180mm lens, f/11.

35: Fujichrome Velvia, 35–70mm zoom lens at 50mm, f/16, tripod.

36–37: Fujichrome Velvia, 35mm lens, f/16, tripod.

38: Fujichrome 100, 35mm lens, f/11 at 1 second.*

39: Fujichrome 50, 35–70mm zoom lens at 35mm, f/8 at 1/15 second, tripod.

40: Ektachrome Professional Plus, 35–135mm zoom lens at 50mm, f/5.6 at 1/30 second.*

41: Fujichrome 50, 38–105mm zoom lens at 50mm.*

42: Fujichrome Velvia, 16mm lens, f/11.

43: Kodachrome 25, 200mm lens, f/11, tripod.

44, **top**: Ektachrome 160T, 21mm lens, f/11.

44, **bottom**: Fujichrome Velvia, 35–70mm zoom lens at 70mm, f/16.

45: Fujichrome 100, 50–250mm zoom

lens at 70mm, f/16 at 4 seconds.

46: Fujichrome 50, 35–70mm zoom lens at 70mm, f/11.

47: Kodachrome 64, 100mm lens, f/4 at 1/250 second.

48: Kodachrome 64, 35–70mm zoom lens at 50mm.*

49: Fujichrome 100, 35–135mm zoom lens at 135mm, f/11.

50: Kodachrome 64, 24mm lens, f/8.

51: Kodachrome 64, 100mm lens, f/8.

52, **opposite**: Fujichrome Velvia, 35–70mm zoom lens at 35mm, f/5.6 at 1/30 second, tripod.

53: Kodachrome 64, 180mm lens, f/8.

54: Kodachrome 64, 90mm macro lens, f/8.

55: Kodachrome 64, 28mm lens, f/8 at 1/30 second.

56: Fujichrome 50, 35–70mm zoom lens at 35mm, f/16, tripod.

57, **left**: Fujichrome Velvia, 35–70mm zoom lens at 35mm, f/11, tripod.

57, **right**: Kodachrome 64, 24mm lens, f/22 at 2 seconds, tripod.

58–59: Fujichrome Velvia, 50–250mm zoom lens at 180mm, f/8 at 1/4 second, tripod.

60: Kodachrome 25, f/16.

61: Fujichrome 50, 35mm lens, f/8, tripod.

62, **top**: Kodachrome 64, 50–250mm zoom lens, f/5.6.

62, **bottom**: Fujichrome 100, 50–250mm zoom lens at 250mm, f/8.

63: Fujichrome 50, 28mm lens, f/16.

64, **top**: Kodachrome 64, 100mm lens, f/8.

64, **bottom**: Kodachrome 64, 24mm lens, f/8.

65: Fujichrome 50, 100mm lens, f/11, tripod.

66: Fujichrome Velvia, 50–250mm zoom lens at 250mm, f/8, tripod.

67: Fujichrome 50, 35mm lens, f/11 at 1/8 second.

68: Fujichrome 100, 50–250mm zoom lens at 200mm, f/16 at 4 seconds.

69, **right**: Fujichrome Velvia, 100mm lens, f/16 at 5 seconds.

70: Fujichrome Velvia, 35–70mm zoom lens at 35mm, f/5.6 at 4 seconds.

71, **top**: Kodachrome 64, 100mm lens,

f/5.6 at 10 seconds.

72, **bottom**: Fujichrome Velvia, 35–70mm zoom lens at 35mm, f/5.6.

72–73: Kodachrome 64, 21mm lens, f/8 at 1/250 second.

74: Fujichrome 50, 300mm lens at f/11.

75: Fujichrome 100, 35–70mm zoom lens at 35mm, f/8.*

76, **left**: Kodachrome 64, 180mm lens, f/5.6 at 1/60 second.

76, **right**: Ektachrome 64, 180mm lens, f/8.

77: Fujichrome 100, 35–70mm zoom lens at 50mm, f/5.6.

78: Fujichrome Velvia, 35–70mm zoom lens at 35mm, f/11, tripod.

79, **left**: Ektachrome 64, 35–70mm zoom lens at 35mm, f/11.

79, **right**: Fujichrome 50, 50–250mm zoom at 250mm, f/22 at 2 seconds.

80: Fujichrome 50, 100mm lens, f/16.

81: Ektachrome EPW, 50–250mm zoom lens at 250mm, f/5.6 at 1/125 second.

82–83: Fujichrome 100, 50–250mm lens at 180mm, f/8, tripod.

84: Fujichrome 100, 28mm lens, f/16, tripod.

85: Kodachrome 64, 24mm lens, f/8.

86, **above**: Fujichrome 100, 35mm lens, f/11.*

86, **below**: Kodachrome 64, 24mm lens, f/8.

87: Kodachrome 64, 35mm lens, f/11.

88–89: Kodachrome 64, 180mm lens, f/8.

89: Kodachrome 64, 100mm lens, f/16.

90: Fujichrome 50, 35–70mm zoom lens at 35mm, f/8.

91, **left**: Kodachrome 25, 24mm lens, f/22.

91, **right**: Fujichrome 50, 35–70mm zoom lens at 35mm, f/16.

92: Fujichrome 50, 50–250mm zoom lens at 250mm, f/16.

93: Kodachrome 64, 35mm lens, f/16.

94, **top**: Fujichrome 50, 35mm lens, f/16, tripod.*

94, **bottom**: Kodachrome 64, 35mm lens, f/4.

95: Fujichrome Velvia, 35–70mm zoom lens at 50mm, f/16, tripod.

96, **left**: Fujichrome 100, 50–250mm zoom lens at 150mm, f/11.

96, **right**: Ektachrome 64, 35–70mm

zoom lens at 35mm, f/8.

97: Kodachrome 64, 24mm lens, f/11.

98, **left**: Fujichrome 100, 28mm lens, f/8.

98, **right**: Kodachrome 64, 100mm lens, f/5.6.

99: Fujichrome 50, 35–70mm zoom lens at 50mm, f/16.*

100, **top**: Fujichrome Velvia, 35–70mm zoom lens at 50mm, f/16, tripod.

100, **bottom**: Fujichrome Velvia, 50–250mm zoom lens at 70mm, f/8.

101: Kodachrome 64, 35mm lens, f/11.

102–103: Fujichrome Velvia, 35–70mm zoom lens at 35mm, f/16, tripod.

104: Kodachrome 64, 180mm lens, f/16, tripod.

105: Fujichrome Velvia, 35–70mm zoom lens at 50mm, f/16 at 2 seconds, tripod.

106: Kodachrome 64, 24mm lens, f/16.

107, **top**: Fujichrome 50, 300mm lens, f/11, tripod.

107, **bottom**: Fujichrome 50, 21mm lens, f/16.

108: Kodachrome 64, 24mm lens, f/16.

109: Kodachrome 64, 35mm lens, f/11.*

110, **left**: Fujichrome Velvia, 28mm lens, f/16.

110, **right**: Kodachrome 64, 28mm lens, f/16.

110, **top**: Kodachrome 64, 50–250mm zoom lens at 250mm, f/8.

111, **bottom**: Kodachrome 64, 180mm lens, f/5.6.

112: Fujichrome 100, 35–70mm zoom lens at 35mm, f/11.

113, **top**: Kodachrome 64, 180mm lens, f/8.

113, **bottom**: Fujichrome Velvia, 35–70mm lens at 50mm, f/11.

114: Kodachrome 64, 35mm lens, f/11.

115: Kodachrome 64, 50–250mm zoom lens at 60mm, f/22.

116–117: Kodachrome 64, 35–70mm zoom lens at 50mm, f/16.

117: Fujichrome 50, 35–70mm zoom lens at 35mm, f/5.6.*

118: Fujichrome Velvia, 35mm lens, f/16, tripod.

119, **top**: Kodachrome 64, 24mm lens, f/16.

119, **bottom**: Fujichrome Velvia, 28mm lens, f/16, tripod.

120: Fujichrome 100, 35–70mm zoom lens at 35mm, f/16, tripod.

121, top: Fujichrome 100, 35–70mm zoom lens at 50mm, f/16, tripod.

121, bottom: Fujichrome 50, 28–48mm zoom lens at 35mm, f/16.

122: Fujichrome 100, 35–70mm zoom lens at 35mm, f/11.*

123: Kodachrome 64, 100mm lens, f/11 at 1 second.

124: Kodachrome 64, 35mm lens, f/11.

125: Ektachrome Professional Plus, 21mm lens, f/16.

126: Fujichrome 50, 35–70mm zoom lens at 35mm, f/16, tripod.

127: Kodachrome 64, 35mm lens, f/11.

128: Kodachrome 64, 24mm lens, f/5.6 at 1/250 second.

129: Fujichrome Velvia, 28mm lens, f/8.

130, top: Fujichrome 100, 35–70mm zoom lens at 35mm, f/11.

130, bottom: Fujichrome 100, 35–70mm zoom lens at 35mm, f/5.6.

130, opposite bottom: Kodachrome 64, 35–70mm zoom lens at 40mm, f/8.*

132: Fujichrome 100, 35mm lens, f/16, tripod.

133: Fujichrome 100, 35–70mm lens at 35mm, f/8.

134: Fujichrome 100, f/16.

135: Fujichrome Velvia, 50–250mm zoom lens at 200mm, f/11.

136–137: Kodachrome 64, 180mm lens, f/4 at 1/125 second.

138: Kodachrome 64, 35mm lens, f/8.

139, top: Ektachrome Professional Plus, f/4 at 1/250 second.

139, bottom: Fujichrome 50, 35–70mm zoom lens, f/11.

140: Ektachrome Professional Plus, 35–70mm zoom lens.*

141: Kodachrome 64, 28mm lens, f/11.

142: Kodachrome 64, 50mm lens, f/5.6.

143: Ektachrome 64, 35–70mm zoom lens at 50mm.*

145: Fujichrome 100, 35–70mm zoom lens at 50mm, f/8.

146: Fujichrome 100, 50–250mm zoom lens, f/5.6.

147, top: Kodachrome 64, 50–250mm zoom lens at 250mm, f/8.

147, bottom: Fujichrome 100, 100mm lens, f/8.

148: Kodachrome 64, 35mm lens, f/11.

149: Kodachrome 64, 180mm lens, f/5.6.

150: Kodachrome 64, 100mm lens at 25-foot distance, f/11.

151: Fujichrome 100, 35mm lens, f/8.

152: Kodachrome 64, 35mm lens at 5 feet, f/8.

153: Fujichrome 100, 35–70mm zoom lens at 35mm, f/8.

154: Kodachrome 64, 35mm lens, f/8.

155: Fujichrome 100, 35–70mm zoom lens at 35mm, f/8.

156: Kodachrome 64, 24mm lens, f/8.

157, top: Kodachrome 64, 35–70mm zoom lens at 70mm, f/8 at 1/125 second.

157, bottom: Kodachrome 64, 28mm lens, f/16.

158, top: Kodachrome 64, 35mm lens, f/8.

158, bottom: Fujichrome 50, 35mm lens, f/8.

159: Fujichrome 100, 50–250mm zoom lens at 170mm, f/8 at 1/125 second.

160: Fujichrome 50, 100mm lens, f/5.6 at 1/250 second.

161: Kodachrome 64, 35mm lens, flash at f/8.

162: Fujichrome 100, 35–70mm lens, f/8.

163: Kodachrome 64, 100mm lens, f/4 at 1/250 second.

164: Kodachrome 64, 35mm lens. f/8.

165: Kodachrome 64, 35–70mm lens, f/5.6.

166, left: Ektachrome EPW, 100mm lens, f/5.6.

166, right: Fujichrome 100, 28mm lens, f/8.

167: Ektachrome 64, 35–70mm zoom lens at 70mm, f/8.

168: Kodachrome 64, 35–70mm zoom lens at 35mm, f/8.

169: Kodachrome 64, 28mm, f/11.

170: Kodachrome 64, 35mm lens, f/16.

171: Kodachrome 64, 35mm lens, f/16.

172–173: Fujichrome Velvia, 28mm lens with polarizing filter, f/16, tripod.

174: Fujichrome 50, 50–250mm zoom lens at 200mm, one stop underexposure for color saturation, f/16.

175, top: Fujichrome 50, 35–70mm zoom lens at 35mm, f/8, tripod.

175, bottom: Fujichrome 100, 21mm lens, 1/2 stop underexposure for color saturation, f/16.

176, top: Ektachrome 64, 50mm lens, metered skyscrapers and underexposed 1 full stop, f/8 at 2 seconds, tripod.

177: Ektachrome Professional Plus, 35–70mm zoom lens, f/11.

178: Fujichrome 100, 50–250mm zoom lens, f/5.6.

179, top: Kodachrome 64, 35mm lens, f/5.6.

179, bottom: Fujichrome 100, 21mm lens, metered monument, f/11.

180: Kodachrome 64, 35mm lens, f/11.

181, top: Kodachrome 64, 50–250mm zoom lens at 200mm, f/8.

181, bottom: Kodachrome 64, 35–70mm zoom lens at 50mm, f/16.

182, top: Kodachrome 64, 35–70mm zoom lens at 70mm, metered stone wall and underexposed 1/2 stop, f/11.

182, bottom: Kodachrome 25, 100mm lens, f/11.

183, top: Fujichrome Velvia, 35mm lens, f/8.

183, bottom: Kodachrome 64, 100mm lens, f/16 at 1/8 second.

184: Fujichrome Velvia, 8mm lens, f/22.

185, top: Kodachrome 200, f/16 at 5 seconds.

185, bottom: Ektachrome 64, 35mm lens, f/5.6.

186: Fujichrome 50, 50mm lens, f/11 at 1/8 second, tripod.

187: Kodachrome 64, 35mm polarized lens, metered counterman in window and shot at reading, f/8.

188: Fujichrome 50, 35–70mm zoom lens at 40mm, f/8.

189: Fujichrome Velvia, 24mm lens, f/16, tripod.

190–191: Kodachrome 64, 24mm lens, f/8 at 1/250 second.

192: Fujichrome 100, 80–200mm lens at 200mm, f/2.8 at 1/15 second.

193, top: Ektachrome 64, 35mm lens, f/8 at 1/30 second.

193, bottom: Kodachrome 64, 28mm lens, f/4 at 1/60 second.

194: Fujichrome 100, 50–250mm lens at 200mm, f/4.

195, top: Fujichrome 100, 50–250mm zoom lens at 150mm, f/8 at 1/250 second.

195, bottom: Kodachrome 64, 24mm lens, f/5.6 at 1/500 second.

196: Fujichrome 100, 35–135mm zoom lens at 35mm, f/8.

197: Ektachrome 64, 100mm lens, f/8.

198: Kodachrome 64, 200mm lens, f/8 at 1/250 second.

199: Fujichrome 100, 28mm lens, f/8.

200: Kodachrome 64, 50mm lens, f/11.

201: Fujichrome 50, 200mm lens, f/8 at 1/250 second.

202: Kodachrome 64, 24mm lens, f/5.6 at 1/500 second.

203: Kodachrome 64, 300mm lens, f/4 at 1/500 second.

204: Fujichrome 100, 200mm lens, f/8 at 1/250 second.

205, top: Fujichrome 100, 500mm lens, f/8.

205, bottom: Fujichrome 100, 50–250mm zoom lens at 250mm, f/8.

206: Fujichrome 50, 28mm lens, f/8 at 1/500 second.

207, top: Kodachrome 64, 24mm lens, f/4 at 1/125 second.

207, bottom: Fujichrome 50, 35–70mm zoom lens at 35mm, f/16 at 1/4 second.

208–209: "sandwich."

210: Ektachrome 64, 35–70mm zoom lens at 35mm.*

211: Fujichrome 100, 100mm lens, f/11.

212: Kodachrome 64, 24mm lens, f/11, tripod.

213: Kodachrome 64, 100mm lens, f/5.6 at 1/125 second.

214, top: Fujichrome 50, 50–250mm zoom lens zooming from 50–150mm, f/8 at 4 seconds.

214, bottom: "sandwich."

215, top: "sandwich."

215, bottom: "sandwich."

INDEX

Page numbers in *italics* refer to illustrations.

PHOTOGRAPHY CREDITS All photographs are credited to Allen Rokach, with the following exceptions: Page 216: NASA, Washington, D.C. Page 217: Collection of the J. Paul Getty Museum, Malibu, California. Page 218, left: Courtesy Daniel Wolf, Inc., New York; Page 218, right: Colorado Historical Society, Denver. Page 219, top left: George Shiras, © National Geographic Society, Washington, D.C.; Page 219, bottom left: The Royal Photographic Society, Bath, England; Page 219, right: Private collection. Page 220, left: Brian Brake/Photo Researchers, Inc., New York; Page 220, top right: Copyright © Jake Rajs, New York; Page 220, bottom right: © Sam Abell.

QUOTATION CREDITS Permission to reproduce quotations has been obtained from the following sources: Page 11: From *When the Going Was Good* by Evelyn Waugh. Reprinted by permission of Little, Brown and Company, Boston; page 82: From *A Concise History of Photography* by Helmut Gernsheim, Dover Publications, Inc., Mineola, New York; page 103: From *The Most Beautiful Place in the World,* introduction by Jay Maisel. © 1986 Jay Maisel, New York; page 137: Susan Kismeric, from a description of "Mean Streets" exhibition, The Museum of Modern Art, New York, 1990. © The Museum of Modern Art. Reprinted by permission; page 173: John Szarkowski, *Looking at Photographs,* The Museum of Modern Art, New York, 1973. © The Museum of Modern Art. Reprinted by permission; page 191: © Henri Cartier-Bresson. Reprinted by permission from *Henri Cartier-Bresson: Aperture Masters of Photography, Number Two,* Aperture, New York, 1987; page 209: © Josef Sudek. Reprinted by permission from *Josef Sudek, Poet of Prague: A Photographer's Life,* Aperture, New York, 1990.